A Novel

Christine

A Life in Germany After WWII
(1945-1948)

*For Mary-Lou
with best wishes
and love,
Johanna Willner*

Johanna Willner

authorHOUSE®

AuthorHouse™
1663 Liberty Drive
Bloomington, IN 47403
www.authorhouse.com
Phone: 1-800-839-8640

First published by AuthorHouse   09/23/2011

ISBN: 978-1-4634-3247-8 (sc)
ISBN: 978-1-4634-3249-2 (hc)
ISBN: 978-1-4634-3248-5 (ebk)

Library of Congress Control Number: 2011911904

Printed in the United States of America

To my wonderful family and friends.

Fences are made for those who cannot fly
Elbert Green Hubbard
(1856-1915)

I would like to thank all the members in my writers groups for their inspiration and encouragement in the completion of this work.

Johanna Willner

Chapter 1

The rolling thunder of artillery fire, so distant only yesterday, had moved closer overnight. Christine Bachmann opened the kitchen window and looked down on the deserted cobblestone street. The brilliant sunlight of the April morning stood in stark contrast to the gloomy mood that lay over Bahrenberg, a small town south of Magdeburg on the Elbe River. March music was blaring from the *Volksempfanger,* the radio controlled by the German government. The tune changed abruptly to the musical theme that always preceded a special report.

"Achtung! Achtung! Das Oberkommando der Wehrmacht gibt bekannt:" President Roosevelt is dead. A miracle has happened. This is the turning point in Germany's destiny. It is an Act of God. The American Soviet alliance is now at the point of breaking up, our scientists have almost completed the wonder weapon that will bring victory to our fatherland.

The march music resumed, only to be interrupted again by a short message to the German troops:

"German soldiers! The Russian tank T-34 is not indestructible. The *Fuhrer* thanks you for your bravery."

The day was April 13, 1945.

Christine turned the knob to silence the aggravating voice, when brother Ulrich appeared, shouting:

"We have to leave it on at all times for special reports and important news. You know that, Christine!" He switched the radio back on, turned around and stomped back to his bedroom.

Mother continued to spread the liquid egg and sugar mixture on the dark slices of heavy bread.

"Mama, we are losing the war," Christine whispered. "I just hope the Americans arrive before the Russians, and that we'll all be alive when that happens. I am only sixteen and I want to live." Her small hands moved her thick brown braids from her chest to the back.

"Christine, Christine, be careful what you say!" Mother urged. "You could be shot for what you just said."

"But it's true," Christine hissed. "That radio is a box full of lies, the refugees are telling the real story." She pushed the radio to the edge of the table. Mother glared at Christine and turned to the younger children, Ruth, eight years old; Gerhard, eleven, and Manfred, just three. Fourteen-year old Ulrich ambled into the kitchen and, without a word, seated himself at the table, grabbing his slice so the liquid would not have time to run off.

Christine left the kitchen, closing the door behind her. She climbed the narrow wooden stairs to the attic. Moments later, she jumped down the stairs, two and three steps at a time. She swung the kitchen door open and shouted:

"Mama, Mama, come quickly, come . . . come!"

Ruth dropped her bread on the table and took Manfred's hand.

"Come on, Manfred, let's run, something is happening," she said, dragging him behind her up the stairs, following the others.

Christine wiped the window pane with her sweater sleeve to clear the dust and spider webs. She moved aside to let Mother look out of the small opening. Pushing her closer to the window, she whispered:

"Do you see those tanks over there, Mama?"

"What about those tanks?"

"Those white stars on the side . . . do you see the white stars, Mama? *Amerikaner . . . ., Amerikaner,* Mama, those are American tanks. The Americans are here."

"Oh, my God," Mother whispered, trembling. "What are we going to do? If only Papa were here, he would know what to do."

"The war is over for us, Mama. No more nights in the cellar. No more air alerts. The Americans are here. We are alive and for us the war is over," Christine said, her voice choking with tears.

Ulrich was still staring at the tanks. Turning around, he said:

"What if they shoot this whole town to bits?" He looked out again.

"They are not moving. They are just sitting there, getting ready."

"We must get a white sheet and hang it out of the window for the Americans to see," Christine suggested, looking around for a white cloth.

"We can't do that, our soldiers will shoot us if we do, they are everywhere around us." Mother said. She was now sitting on an old mattress, her hands folded in her lap. The younger children were playing with broken toys.

"But we must," Christine urged, "or the Americans think this town will fight and they'll shoot this place up."

"They are moving, they are moving!" Ulrich shouted. "The Americans are coming to Bahrenberg."

More and more American military vehicles appeared on the distant road, the main highway connecting Halberstadt with Magdeburg. There was still no sign of life in the streets of Bahrenberg, gray stone structures along cobblestone streets, a ghost town.

"The mayor is raising a white flag," Christine called out, pointing to an attic window a few houses away where a bed sheet was slowly being hoisted. As if the people of Bahrenberg had been waiting for this signal, more and more sheets and pillow cases appeared.

The American tanks entered Bahrenberg from the east, crossing the railroad tracks just outside town. They encountered no resistance and drove straight into *Adolf-Hitler-Strasse*, the main street, the street where the Bachmanns lived. Christine and her family were now watching the Americans from behind the living room curtains.

"Gosh," Ruth sighed, pressing her face against the window. "I wish I were older!"

"Yeah, right out of Hollywood," Ulrich teased. "Why don't you girls go down and introduce yourselves?"

"Oh, please, Mama, please, may we go?" Ruth chirped. "Look, everybody is coming out!"

"No, you stay here," Mother ordered. "It is not safe out there, we have to wait and see."

"But look, Mama," Christine said. "The soldiers are smiling and talking to the children."

"All right, all right, but stay close to the gate and away from the vehicles."

Ulrich, Gerhard and Ruth raced down the stairway. Christine, holding Manfred's hand, followed slowly. A soldier called from a tank:

"Want some chocolate?" He bent down and stretched his arm to offer a chocolate bar to the nearest boy, about ten years old. The boy looked at the soldier, then at the chocolate. He kept his hands in the pockets of his trousers that showed bare knees through big holes. The other children stared. The soldier unwrapped the chocolate and started to eat it. He held the other half toward the children, but the children stared at the soldier as he finished the chocolate himself.

Another soldier stepped from a jeep and ambled toward the group with a friendly grin:

"How 'bout a piece of gum?"

Silence. Then a small voice: "Was ist gum?"

The soldier smiled at the little boy with the thick brown hair and large gray eyes, his upper two front teeth missing. The little boy looked embarrassed, the other children giggled. The soldier squatted down:

"What's your name, sonny?"

"Willy."

"O.k., Willy. You don't know what gum is? Let me show you!"

He took a small gray strip from a green wrapper, pushed it into his mouth and started chewing, his jaws moving with exaggeration. Other soldiers had joined in the demonstration.

"Like cows," Ulrich whispered behind his cupped hand.

The soldier rose. "You see, and after you have chewed it for a while, you spit it out, just like this." He spit the gray mass as far as he could into the street. The children looked at each other and laughed.

"That was funny," Ruth turned to Christine. "But why do they chew that stuff and then spit it out? What would anyone want to do that for?"

All through the war the German people had been told that the Americans would kill children with poisoned chocolates. No, these men would not kill children. Christine just knew.

The sound of a heavy explosion interrupted the unfolding friendships between the American soldiers and the German children. The children darted into their homes. The Americans restarted their vehicles, backed into the narrow side street and sped away in the direction from which they had come. Explosions like fire crackers alternated with heavy detonations.

Mother, pillows and blankets in her arms, came rushing down the stairs as the children ran up:

"I knew it . . . I knew it . . ." she said. "We are not safe, who knows what they . . ." She tried to stop the children from running up. "Everybody get in the cellar at once! Christine, carry Manfred . . . Ruth, Ulrich, Gerhard, let's go!"

"No," Christine shouted, pushing Mother back upstairs. "No, we are not going back into that cellar. I always hated it, always thought that someday the whole house would come down on us, burying us all alive. I'd rather be hit by a bomb."

She strode upstairs, everybody, including Mother, following her.

"Sorry, I shouted, Mother," Christine said, turning around briefly. She had heard Mother weeping in her room many nights after the children had gone to bed. "But the Americans are here. They'll take care of us."

The explosions had subsided.

An agonizing scream tore the silence. A woman came running around the bend. Christine rushed downstairs.

"Mrs. Brenner, Mrs. Brenner, what . . ."

"Guuunterrr, Guuunterrr . . . !" The desperation chilled the air. She stopped briefly, catching her breath as she lifted her pregnant belly.

"Gunter . . . I'm looking for Gunter. Have you seen him? You must have seen him and the Bergmann twins and Erich Kroner just coming by here a few minutes ago. They wanted to welcome the Americans, I couldn't hold them back. You must have seen them!" She wiped the perspiration from her forehead with the back of her hand.

Christine shook her head.

"They left when the white sheets went up." Mrs. Brenner said, turned around and started to run again; and again that haunting scream:

"Guunnter . . . Guunnnter!"

Meanwhile, the American tanks and jeeps had arrived at the scene of the explosions, a deserted German military freight train on the railroad tracks they had passed only half an hour before. They could not get close. Other US military vehicles on their way to Bahrenberg had rushed to the scene at the first sound of detonations. They had blocked off the area and had quickly disconnected the exploding railroad car, pushing the other three away.

They saw a boy sitting in the grass. They jumped from their vehicles and ran towards him. He stared at them in a daze.

" . . . anyone in there?"

The boy held up three fingers and nodded, coughing in the dense smoke. Several soldiers jumped on the train and disappeared inside, disregarding the increasing violent flames and detonations.

"His feet are blown off," a soldier shouted, jumping from the train, holding a small body against his bloodstained chest.

"Quick, get the tourniquets!"

" . . . To the aid station!"

"This one, too, he is in shock." Another soldier followed the first one. The jeep with the two soldiers carrying their human load sped off toward the highway and disappeared from sight.

"The flames are reaching the big stuff," a soldier shouted as he leaped from the train. "Let's get the hell out of here. There is no one alive in there."

He grabbed the boy's arm, pulling him along, shouting: "Let's go, let's go!" At a safe distance he released the boy and wiped his forehead with his uniform sleeve. Within seconds the railroad car was engulfed in flames, leaving only the steel frame on the tracks.

"*Wie heisst du?*" asked the American soldier in halting German.

"Erich."

"How old are you?"

"Fourteen."

"What happened?"

"Well, we went in there; and . . . and I found this hand grenade, and I told them I knew how to throw it and—and-they laughed. And I took it, and I jumped from the train. And then I threw it into the train, just to show them . . . that's when it all started."

"Where did you learn to throw that thing?"

"In the *Volkssturm.*"

Mrs. Brenner ran towards Erich, screaming and close to collapsing.

"Where is he?" Erich looked at her and at the train.

A soldier caught her as she fainted; others helped him carry her to a jeep. An hour later she gave birth to a son at the American aid station.

Chapter 2

For the first time in months the Bachmanns slept upstairs. The rumbling of military vehicles on the cobblestones kept them up most of the night. But it was a comforting sound. For the first time in years they felt secure.

A fire roaring in the iron living room stove brought Christine from the bedroom long before dawn.

"I've been up since three o'clock," Mother said without looking up. Perched on a little stool, she was hacking away at a portrait of *Fuhrer* Adolf Hitler, a fixture in every German household. One by one she fed the little strips into the fire that eased the April morning chill.

"We should keep the frame," Christine suggested, sitting down by the stove. "Who knows when we'll ever get a good frame like this again." She rubbed her hands together, trying to remember when this stove had been lit the last time. All through winter there had been no fuel.

"Everything goes," Mother said, her face tensing in an increased effort to cut the oak wood. "The frame would only remind us of the picture that was in it." She paused briefly, leaning back.

"I just hope I am doing the right thing. If the Americans move out again, we'll be in deep trouble. I don't even want to think about it." She started hacking again. "But now this can only help us. If the Americans find this stuff, they think we all loved the *Fuhrer.*"

"Look at this, the Bible of the Third Reich! And just think that no one in this family ever read it!" She held up Hitler's *Mein Kampf,* the book Hitler had written about his struggles, and which, like his portrait, had to be part of every German household. She ripped it apart and fed the pages into the fire. The flames increased and danced around, curling up the paper, swallowing it with a hissing sound.

Christine moved to the window and watched the activities in the streets. American troops in jeeps, tanks and trucks, loaded with men and military equipment, were moving around. Soldiers tended to their duties, others stood around, chatting and laughing. Former slave laborers, mainly Poles and Ukrainians, brought to Germany by the Nazi government to work in factories and fields tried to make friends with their liberators. They were free now and refused to work for their former German masters. Few German adults were in the street.

The water kettle on the stove gave off a high pitched whistle and brought the younger siblings from their bedroom. Mother carried the boiling water to the kitchen. She took a handful of roasted grain from a tin marked "*Kaffee*" and slid it into the top of the square wooden coffee mill. When the crackling noise turned into a smooth humming sound, she stopped the handle. She opened the little drawer at the bottom of the mill and poured the light brown powder into the white china coffee pot, adding boiling water. Soon the liquid looked dark enough, coffee was ready. Mother tried to get the bread slices with the egg and sugar mixture quickly into the eager little hands.

Sipping the tasteless liquid, Christine wondered how life would go on. With Papa being away, life had already changed. He had never tolerated thoughts and ideas other than his own. Any questions and doubts Christine and Harald, only one year older than she, had voiced, had always been shot down in a harsh voice:

"You don't understand. You are too young!" And when they had expressed their fear of the fighting coming closer from all sides, he had just shouted:

"I won't tolerate this kind of talk in this house. Do you want us all end up in . . ." and he had stalked off to the library, slamming the door behind him.

Now there was peace in the home. Mother had become stronger, less afraid to follow her own instincts. And, secretly, the children were all hoping that it would stay like this for a while longer. But Harald must come back soon, Christine thought. Only 17 years old, and in his last grade of high school, he and all his classmates had been drafted into the army at the end of 1944. The family had not heard from him since he left.

A sharp knock at the apartment door interrupted Christine's thoughts. Mother opened carefully.

"Christine!" Gerda Werner, a neighbor, rushed into the kitchen. Carrying a bucket with shopping nets in each hand, she shouted:

"Let's go, Christine! Haven't you heard? There is a freight train on the tracks behind the Ottersberg Estate . . . with oil and yarn. Come on, let's go! Everybody is out there, some are already coming back." She pointed out of the kitchen window.

"You can't just go there and take things from the train," Mother interrupted. "You could be shot."

"The Americans have opened it, and they are there, too. It's a German military supply train, they say, a train that didn't make it to the front. Well, I guess, this is the front, I mean to the German soldiers. Let's go before everything is gone!" Gerda said.

"Christine is not going," Mother said in a firm voice without looking up. "It's too dangerous out there. The Americans don't have things under control yet, and the foreign laborers are very angry at us for having been forced to work for Germany. Who knows what they will do to you when the Americans are not looking."

"I'm going," Christine said, bringing two *rucksacks* and two buckets from the storage room. Throwing one *rucksack* to Ulrich, she said,

"And you too, Ulrich, we need strong arms."

Ulrich disappeared in the bedroom and returned quickly, still buttoning his trousers. They strapped their *rucksacks* to their backs, grabbed the buckets and rushed down the stairs.

They joined the stream of people moving along *Adolf-Hitler-Strasse,* women, children, and a few old men. The Americans watched the serious colorless mass in silence, faintly returning the smiles of the children. Old men tipped their hats as they passed American soldiers. Some soldiers returned the salute awkwardly. At the farthest end of the street, just before *Adolf-Hitler Strasse* turned into the wide dirt road leading to the railroad tracks, military police jeeps and ambulances crowded the entrance way to the Ottersberg Estate, the largest farm property for miles.

"Looks like the Americans are going to use that place as their headquarters," Ulrich said, "or as a hospital. Look, there are ambulances over there!"

"Move on . . . move on!" an MP shouted, clearly agitated by the slow moving crowd.

"What's going on?" Ulrich had spotted his classmate Hans.

"Shooting, there are shots coming out of the cellar. They say there are *Volkssturm* people in there, or German soldiers."

Shots like firecrackers came from the cellar window at the end of the building. The American soldiers darted in various directions to encircle the area. The MPs tried to push the curious crowd back into the street.

"Get back—get back!" They shouted, but the people just stood and waited.

An MP shot in the air. The young people ran behind houses and trees, leaving the old ones confused and scared.

More shots came from the cellar. Then a shrill voice:

"Go back to America, barbarians, I'll kill you all!" Another round of shots followed. More soldiers ran toward the main house with readied guns.

"Oh, my God, my God!" a woman shrieked. "They are blowing up the place with all the people inside—oh, my God!" She turned around and ran back to the street.

A tall man stumbled toward the soldiers, trying to keep his hands high in the air.

"Don't shoot, don't shoot," someone screamed. "It's the Count, the Count, oh, God, don't shoot the Count!"

Count Bodo von Ottersberg fell exhausted to the ground, his arms awkwardly stretched into the air. "It's my mother," he said.

An MP grabbed Count Bodo by his arm, lifted him to his feet, and pulled him back toward the house. Other soldiers followed close behind. A few isolated shots came from the window.

"Move on! Move on!" Several MPs moved towards the crowd, shouting, anger in their voices, when they saw that the people did not want to move.

Christine was glad to see American soldiers patrolling the train area.

"Hello, how do you do?" Ulrich practiced his third-year English on any American willing to listen. "It's a fine day," he continued when his smile was returned.

The line by the oil moved quickly. An old woman waddled towards them, struggling with two half-filled buckets.

"What kind of oil is it?" Christine asked.

"You want to try it?" the woman offered, setting her load down. She stuck her index finger into the thick yellow liquid and licked it.

" . . . tastes like rapeseed oil," the woman said, nodding. "Guess we can't expect to get poppy seed oil if we get it that cheap." She chuckled. "At least it's not machine oil. It's food."

She picked up her load and moved on. Christine and Gerda filled their buckets and carried them away from the train.

"Ulrich, you stay here and guard the oil with your life," Christine said, arranging the containers close to Ulrich. "We'll see what's over there."

The American soldiers had organized the distribution of large olive drab and white spools of cotton yarn. One soldier leaned out of the wide train opening.

"Here, little ladies," he called out. "Take it! It's all yours, a present from the *Fuhrer!*" He clowned around, struggling with the German pronunciation, and continued to throw the spools playfully at the girls and women who could hardly keep up with the speed.

That night the aroma of potatoes fried in rapeseed oil lay like a heavy cloud over Bahrenberg.

Chapter 3

The bulk of the American forces had moved on to Magdeburg. A small military compound had been established at the Ottersberg Estate. Through a bullhorn the citizens of Bahrenberg were told that they must get daily information on occupation rules and regulations from the bulletin board at the city hall. Failure to abide by the rules would be severely punished. The mayor and his staff, except for political appointees, would continue to function under the supervision of the American military government until changes could be made. The current ration cards would remain in effect. The radio brought only music from the American Armed Forces Network.

Spring planting, already late, was the first priority. All citizens were ordered to register and it was determined that all able-bodied citizens 12 years and older had to work in the fields. Former slave laborers refused to work, but were told that they had to in order to get ration cards. Many moved on to western Germany in the hope to get to America. Others wanted to go back to their homelands in the east.

Masses of refugees, mainly ethnic Germans, expelled by the Russian and Polish governments, tired women, children, and old men, struggled through Bahrenberg on their way to the west. They claimed that the Russians were just a few hours behind them and urged the Poles and Ukrainians not to go back, but rather find a new home in the west.

"Your homes are destroyed," they said. "We saw it all. And the Russian hordes will come here too. Surely they will come."

And they hurried on, carrying small bundles with bare necessities. A few months earlier they had left their homes in East Prussia, Pomerania, Silesia and districts in the Polish border areas on covered wagons with all the household goods they could transport. They had lost everything. Many people had died on the road from exhaustion, starvation, attacks by low-flying British and Russian planes, bombings and disease.

"We should go with the refugees to the west," Christine suggested, as she looked down on the stream of refugees moving slowly along *Adolf-Hitler-Strasse.* "What if the Russians come here and we are stuck with them?"

Mother shook her head.

"They won't. The Americans will not give up what they have." She fumbled with her apron. "Besides, we cannot leave here. Papa and Harold would not find us when they return from the war. Our family belongs here, together."

Every morning men in civilian clothing with white armbands, a sign of their official function, tacked information bulletins to the wooden board outside the mayor's office, with daily instructions, regulations, and information the new government had decided the citizens should know. There was no information on what was happening in the rest of the country. Mail and telephone service for private citizens had not resumed, no newspaper was being published.

"Good news for you, Ulrich, schools will be closed indefinitely," Christine said, returning from the information board.

"You mean we'll never have to go to school again?" piped Gerhard, his eyes lighting up. "But then we won't need teachers anymore, so what will Papa do when he comes back?"

Christine sat down and read the long directive, Proclamation I, signed by General Eisenhower. A tightly written statement informed the German population of Eisenhower's plans to govern the area under his command and ordered the people to abide by the rules set forth therein.

The Allied military government was now in charge of the German courts. Local government officials were to remain at their posts until changes would be announced. The farm work would continue without interruption. Schools were tentatively scheduled to reopen 1 September 1945. Curfew, established between 10:00pm and 6:00am would remain in effect until further notice.

All weapons, ammunitions, explosives, and radio transmitters had to be turned in. No German was permitted to leave the area beyond five kilometers without a special permit. Old ration cards would remain in effect until new ones could be issued. People working in the cities of Schoenebeck and Magdeburg would be issued special permits, allowing them to be on the streets early in the morning and late at night for travel to and from work and during special shifts. Gatherings of more than five adults were prohibited except in food queues or for church services. During the registration each person was issued an identification card which he had to carry with him at all times. The registration would become the basis for the issuance of five groups of ration cards. Class 1 was the highest group, with 1800 calories a day, issued to people engaged in heavy work. Class 5, for non-working people, was generally called the "*Hungerkarte*," or "cemetery ration," with 800 calories, which everybody tried to avoid, because it "wasn't enough to live on but too much to die." Every adult was handed a questionnaire, the *Fragebogen*, which required the respondent to list all his memberships in the National Socialist and military organizations, as well as salary, associations and employment back to pre-Hitler years. With this *Fragebogen* the military government hoped to detect not only overt Nazi supporters but also sympathizers, militarists, and other individuals who had benefited from the Nazi regime.

No "big Nazi" showed up at the registration in Bahrenberg. No German or even an angry slave laborer could point out a single real Nazi in this town. Yet almost everyone was a member of a Nazi organization, the men of the *Partei*, the National Socialist Party; the women of the women's movement, the *Frauenschaft*, and the children, down to the age of ten, of the Hitler Youth. Many people claimed later that they had joined the Party merely to protect themselves. If they saw an injustice done, they just looked the other way and never mentioned it to anyone. Adults had learned not to trust each other, even within the family. Children, in a harmless chatter, could pass on to other people what they had heard at home, and that could have disastrous consequences.

The people lived a simple life. They worked, ate and slept. On weekends the young people enjoyed the Saturday night dances at the *Gasthaus*, where, in a few smaller rooms, the men played cards and drank beer and cognac. The women stayed home with the children. After the children had gone to bed, the mothers would knit or sew and listen to a story or play on the radio that was constructed in such a way that no foreign station could be received. This had been Goebbels' idea about which he had bragged at many parties.

The area around Magdeburg had always been a "Red" area, with a strong Socialist and Communist history. Thus the Nazis had selected outsiders to watch over the activities in Bahrenberg. Christine remembered how strongly Papa had resisted the move to Bahrenberg two years earlier. He claimed that the transfer had been punishment for a remark he had made during a card game about the deterioration of the war situation. He never found out.

"I can't move to that Communist infested area again," he had shouted. As a young teacher he had lived, for almost ten years, in the village of Saaldorf on the Saale, only forty kilometers from Bahrenberg. The clatter of the nailed boots of Hitler's Brownshirts and the Communists chasing each other in the night, beating each other with night sticks, and the screams of the victims, were still vivid in his mind. Christine, who was born in Saaldorf, and who had spent the first six years of her life there, had only pleasant memories of the village. On summer afternoons, she and her friends would sit by the bank of the Saale, waving to the boats men on the tugs. And the boys would shout: "Where ya going?" and the boats men would call back: "To America." And they would disappear around the bend where the Saale soon joins the Elbe.

And the winters! She would never forget the winters in Saaldorf. In the early evenings the children would trot to the village hill as large snowflakes drifted through the air. The lights in the windows would appear, one by one, and the night watchman would walk around, lighting the gaslights in the street. The aroma of apples baking in the tile ovens spilled into the street and mingled with the moist fragrance of snow and pine needles. Wrapped in bulky coats and struggling through the snow in their heavy boots, their woolen caps and mittens knit by their mothers or grandmothers, the children would drag their homemade sleds behind them on a string, wooden crates, cut open on one broad side by their fathers or grandfathers, the open edge equipped with metal strips, rounded in the front. And they would stand in line, awaiting their turn to race down the hill, jumping from one foot to the other and curling their little fingers in their mittens, hoping that moving their fingers and toes would keep them from freezing before the real fun started. The sleds with the metal strips were the fastest. The younger timid ones would turn their box around and sit in it, protected from two sides. They were much slower, but since they were often pushed by those sailing down at high speed, they, too, made it to the bottom of the hill, everyone screaming with delight.

One day in 1934, Papa had told the family that they were moving to Rastenbeck in northern Germany, a small village in the Altmark, not far from where their grandparents lived.

"Rastenbeck was built in the middle ages," he had said. "The houses surround the town square in horseshoe shape, with the fronts facing the square. This way the villagers could better defend their homes. The "horseshoe's" open end faces the main throughway, an unpaved road connecting Rastenbeck with Altendorf and Siebenstadt. The church register will tell us much about the history. The school house was built later outside the circle, along with other dwellings housing newcomers, outsiders."

"Look at those woods, children . . . those oaks . . . they must be many hundreds of years old!" Papa had said as they were entering Rastenbeck in a horse drawn carriage provided by the mayor. "It's in nature where the real life is. Look at those fields, the golden grain swaying gently as if touched by the hand of God!" And they had waved at a woman walking along the edge of a field with her young daughter who was wearing a wreath of deep-blue cornflowers on her blond curls and holding a bunch of tired poppies in her tiny hand.

The people of Rastenbeck lived by the natural cycle of time. The rituals of the seasons occupied a large part of their days. They saw God as a benevolent father, strict but fair. If they did their best to live by the commandments, He, in turn, would give them the good life. If tragedy struck or a problem arose, they dealt with them as best they could. Perhaps God was punishing them for something they had done. Twice a month a Lutheran pastor came from Siebenstadt for services at the small church, built with field rocks hundreds of years ago. The whole village rejoiced in the birth of a child and celebrated a wedding. Adults and children joined the procession of a departed to the cemetery outside the town. The old graveyard surrounding the church had run out of space long ago. The children grew up to continue their fathers' work. Generation followed generation. There was closeness in the families and harmony in the community. Karl Bachmann, now Rastenbeck's sole teacher, soon served as the church organist. Much of his spare time he and his family spent cultivating vegetables and berries, new fruit trees and tending to his bees.

One day a new family moved to Rastenbeck, a man named Vogel, with his wife and son. Their newly built home was at the edge of town, on the road to Siebenstadt. For a while they seldom came down to the village. People talked about them in a low voice.

"He looks like a mean bird," the children would whisper. "And his boy looks just like him."

One day Mother passed Mrs. Vogel on the street. She approached to greet her, but noticing Mrs. Vogel's tightly pressed thin lips and averted eyes, she only nodded with the trace of a smile and moved on.

"We have to watch out for these people, they look evil," the adults would tell each other. And when Mr. Vogel joined the men on Saturday night for a card game at the *Gasthaus,* the laughs became awkward and soon no one spoke. After a few weeks he stopped coming.

"Mr. Vogel visited Mayor Schulz today," Papa said during the noon meal after school. "He says that all those who have not joined the Party yet should do so. He is the *Ortgruppenleiter,* the district leader, for this area. He says that the *Fuhrer* has done so much for Germany already, and that it is important that we all support him. Adolf Hitler has shown how he loves the German people by endangering his life; by giving the people work and hope and enough to eat; by making Germany stronger every day; by restoring self-respect in the German people that was crushed by the Versailles Treaty!"

Papa paused.

"Mr. Vogel also says: "The *Fuhrer* will give us an army that can conquer the world, and with the German people behind him, we all can reach for the stars. Of course, nobody has to join the Party. It is all a free choice. The *Fuhrer* need not exert pressure, his actions speak for themselves."

Soon thereafter Mr. Vogel visited the Bachmanns who lived in one wing of the small schoolhouse. And after he had left, that day in 1936, Papa, an employee of the state, of course, he, too, had a free choice, 'but it would be advisable,' became a member of the *Fuhrer's* team, the National Socialist German Workers Party, the NSDAP. Instead of soft music, the radio brought marching music and fiery speeches. And Papa listened to them, chewing on wooden matches and shaking his head. And there were no more political discussions while the children were around.

Mr. Vogel visited the Bachmanns more often. He rode around the village on his bicycle, this tall, lanky man, his long neck topped by a small bird face under cropped blond hair. Looking left and right, he clearly enjoyed his powerful position. On one of his visits he told Papa he needed someone to collect the dues from Party members, and since Papa, Mr. Vogel said, was intelligent and reliable, he became the district treasurer for the Party.

"So everybody in town is a member now?" Papa asked Mr. Vogel.

"Everybody except that scum Richter, but we'll take care of that parasite, that Communist."

Christine, playing with her cut-out paper dolls under the table, wondered why that nice Mr. Richter, Paul's father, was called such a bad name. But she felt it was better not to ask Papa.

On September 1, 1939, German troops marched into Poland, "after being provoked," the radio announcer shouted, "to the point where the *Fuhrer* had no choice." When the troops returned three weeks later, the school children were sent with flowers to the highway that passed 2km north of Rastenbeck, to welcome the returning heroes.

Christine, too, threw her bouquet of asters on one of the open trucks filled with soldiers. The soldiers waved and smiled and soon disappeared in the distance.

A few days later, the first twenty Polish prisoners-of-war were brought to Rastenbeck. They were housed in one of the vacant cottages Mayor Schulz provided for his laborers. The cottage had quickly been surrounded by a barbed wire fence, installed on the weekend by the village men.

Christine, looking through the fence in the evening when the men had returned from the fields, was surprised that they did not look like monsters at all. They smiled at her and did not look any different from other people she knew. Whenever Mother baked a cake, Christine secretly wrapped a few pieces into old newspapers, stashed them into her apron pocket, and went to the cottage. There she pushed the package through the fence for any prisoner who happened to pass. She stopped going when Papa told her that Mr. Vogel had forbidden for anyone to 'go near that place.'

"Mr. Vogel can't order people around," Harald had said. "He is not the mayor."

"Mr. Vogel is the most powerful man in this town now," Papa said, turning around, indicating that the conversation was finished.

Mr. Vogel introduced the Hitler salute soon after his arrival in Rastenbeck. He insisted that the right arm be raised high. People who gave him a sluggish salute had to come back and present the proper gesture. When he ordered the prisoners-of-war on their way to the field to salute, some laughed and went on, until one day Mr. Vogel brought his whip and beat an offender unconscious. From that day on Mr. Vogel always brought his whip and everybody saluted him in the proper manner.

As time went on, the Polish prisoners were replaced by Belgians, French and civilian laborers from Poland and Russia, called *Ostarbeiter.* The people of Rastenberg lived their lives like before and, except for "the good news of constant victories," were untouched by the war during the first two years. Only Mr. Richter had been drafted into the army as soon as the war started. He had "died for *Fuhrer* and Fatherland on the field of honor," so it said in the district paper where every obituary of a fallen soldier was marked with an iron cross. Before Christmas Mrs. Richter and Paul moved away and were not heard from again.

As the victorious German army occupied one European country after another, people all over the country rejoiced. There was not enough space in the newspapers to print all the exciting news. Hitler and Goebbels made speeches all the time. And the school children had to listen to all of them. And when the speeches were over, the children had to stand up, raise their arm high in the Hitler salute and sing the national anthem, *Deutschland, Deutschland, ueber alles,* and the *Horst Wessel* song, the Party song, *Die Fahne hoch.* Special reports, preceded by classical music themes and military marches, chased one another. The radio was blaring constantly, and when Mother told Papa to "turn that thing down," he shouted:

"Don't you want to hear the good news?"

And Mother had gone to the bedroom, crying. Christine had followed her, trying to calm her.

"He is just happy about all the good news," she had said.

After a long moment of silence, Mother said, making every word count: "Christine, your father . . . has . . . gone . . . mad!"

Christine could never forget that moment that had changed her life. The feeling of comfort and security was gone.

Delirium had gripped the masses. Shouts, screams, and blaring music had chipped away at the sensitivity of the people, finally killing it in many of them.

Chapter 4

Christine walked with her family to the registration office. She wondered what Papa would answer if asked about his Nazi past. Yes, he had been a member of the Party. No, he did not consider himself a Nazi. Yes, he had been Mr. Vogel's treasurer for a while. And she thought of the time when Mr. Vogel had beaten the Polish laborer, whom everybody knew by the name of Antek. Papa had done nothing, neither had the other people in Rastenbeck who had seen the attack or heard about it. Shouldn't they all have taken the whip from Mr. Vogel and beaten him to death? Or had they been afraid that Mr. Vogel could quickly be replaced by others like him; or that the Party officials would come and punish the whole village? And where had God been? Why didn't He strike Mr. Vogel dead? He couldn't have been on Mr. Vogel's side! *Gott Mit Uns*—God With Us—was engraved on the belt buckles of the German soldiers. What kind of God kept silent when an injustice was done, when an innocent human being was made to suffer? Had Papa and the others feared the Nazis more than God? Yes, they were afraid of the very people who espoused superior character, pride, and honor, afraid of the people who had promised the good life for everyone. Was that the reason so many people had joined the Party, out of fear? What was Nazism all about? How many people had actually read Hitler's book *Mein Kampf*, his account of his philosophy and early struggles? People wanted to believe the promise of the good life. They wanted work and leisure in good balance. They wanted security. Having your children join the Hitler Youth groups, where the bright and cunning youngsters quickly advanced to leadership positions, now meant security. And now they would have to answer for their actions.

Mr. Alpert, the school principal, and Mr. Kohler, the mayor, were conducting the registration in the presence of a young American officer. Several MPs—American Military Police—were standing against the back wall, their weapons slung over their shoulders. Mr. Alpert went to great length explaining the registration form, urging people to think carefully before writing anything down. False statements, he said, would result in severe punishment.

"It's better not to write anything if you are not sure or can't remember," he said. "They'll be able to find the information somewhere, and if you lie, you'll surely suffer."

"What about my father and Harald?" Christine asked. "We have not heard from them for months."

Mr. Alpert pointed to a space on top of the page.

"Just write your father's name here, as head of the household, and Harald's as the first child. They just report in when they return from the war."

Mr. Kohler had already sorted out the ration cards for the Bachmann family as he was waiting for Christine to finish registering all family members.

"Hello, Manfred!" he bent down to shake Manfred's hand. "You are getting to be a big boy now. Your Papa won't recognize you when he returns." He stroked Manfred's carefully groomed hair. "How old are you now?"

Manfred counted four fingers on his right hand and held them up to Mr. Kohler.

"Four years old?" Mr. Kohler smiled.

"Almost," Christine said.

Mr. Kohler nodded. He picked up the ration cards.

"Working rations for Ulrich, Christine, and you, Mrs. Bachmann, here they are."

"I don't intend to work in the fields," Mother said in a low voice. "I plan to take care of my younger children."

"But then I must give you the bad card, Category No. 5. Perhaps you can work for a few hours a day where you can take the children or find someone to take care of Manfred, some old woman, perhaps?"

"No, I'd rather not. We'll be alright."

"Are you sure?"

Mother nodded.

Mr. Kohler watched Mother gather the ration cards and stash them into her ragged brown purse with the broken lock.

"Christine, Ulrich, you start working at our place on Monday morning at 7 o'clock," he said.

He leaned over to Mother and said:

"We'll try to help where we can, it won't be easy."

"Thank you, *Herr Buergermeister,*" Christine said as she turned to leave, her family following her. She wondered what Mr. Kohler had meant by trying to help.

"That's over," Mr. Kohler said, holding out his hand to say goodbye. "I am not the mayor anymore, Mr. Krieger is."

"Mr. Krieger—the barber? That can't be! He is over 80 years old. That's impossible!" Christine's voice was louder than she had intended.

"He is the only one without any trace of Nazism in his past," Mr. Kohler said under his breath. "He says he has always been a Communist. I don't think the Americans like the situation, but at least they can be sure, he was not a Nazi. But he is just a figure head. After all, the Americans are running this town now."

Ulrich opened the heavy oak door and let the family file past him.

"Oh, my God," Mother whispered. "Did you see what I was just about to do? Raise my right arm in the Hitler salute! It's become so automatic. Oh, my God! I wonder if the policemen by the wall noticed anything." She glanced back. But the MP's just stood there, chewing gum, looking at no one and nothing in particular.

American soldiers were chatting outside the building. Looking at the Bachmanns, they stopped talking. A soldier, with a slightly olive skin and a trace of a beard, the rim of his helmet stopping just above the heavy eyebrows under which large gentle eyes sparkled at Christine, quickly pushed a little brown bag into Christine's hand. She pushed it back and he handed it to Manfred, turned around and rushed back to his comrades. No one spoke. After a few steps Manfred opened the bag.

"Look what's in here," he called out, lifting out a piece of the whitest bread they had ever seen.

"Is that real?" Ulrich touched the bread gently. "Do you think Americans eat that all the time?" They all touched it. "It's so soft, so white . . ."

" . . . remember that poem we had to learn at school, Ulrich? The one that said in part: I'd rather live in misery in

Germany than eat white bread in a foreign land? I wonder who wrote that, but I would have gladly eaten white bread in a foreign land . . ."

"Me, too!" chirped Ruth. "Can we eat it now?"

"Eat it! Eat it!" Manfred shouted, holding up the bread.

"No, we'll eat that at home," Christine said, putting the bread back into the bag. "Things like that must be enjoyed." She closed the bag and carried it herself.

American military policemen and Polish civilians employed by the Americans were crowding the school grounds.

"What's going on?" Christine asked Janek, a young Pole who had worked for the Kohlers.

He pointed to the classroom just below the Bachmann's living room.

"This classroom is the collection point for guns and ammunition and all that stuff."

Christine peeked through the window.

"Isn't it dangerous the way they are doing this, smoking cigarettes and handling guns and ammunition? You know, they could blow up this place and we are right above."

Janek shrugged his shoulders. "Why should I care," he mumbled.

Christine stomped away and followed the others upstairs. Through the open window she could hear an American soldier calling through the bullhorn for people to turn in their weapons immediately, otherwise all houses would be searched. More people rushed to the school house, handed in closed bags and left quickly.

In the afternoon, as the family sat around the kitchen table playing cards, there was a knock on the door. Mother opened carefully.

"Christine, come her at once!" she called back, her voice shaking with fear.

An American officer and several military policemen walked into the apartment. Christine led them past the kitchen to the living room. Mother followed quickly. The officer said in a German free of a foreign accent:

"I am Captain Berger. We need your apartment, in fact, the whole building for three days. We want you to be out in two hours. Take anything you need and don't forget your valuables!" He looked around, then at his watch. It's three o'clock now. Be sure to be out by five."

He turned to go.

"Oh, my God, two hours," Mother wailed. "How can we do that in two hours? Isn't there a chance we can stay just in one room? This is just terrible."

Captain Berger turned back briefly, gave Mother an icy stare and headed for the door.

"Sergeant Hutchinson," he shouted. "I want you to move in your men at five o'clock sharp!"

As the men were leaving, Mother wiped her eyes with the corner of her apron.

"Ulrich, run over to the Alperts and ask if we can stay with them for three days," Christine took over. "We can't waste another minute."

Ulrich skipped down the stairs. Mother and Christine began to gather clothing and food. The younger children filled their school satchels with toys and story books. Mother looked through the desk drawers for any Nazi evidence, fearing that the Americans might smash the furniture if they found anything, as she had heard had happened in other homes. At 4:45pm she turned the key and left it in the lock, just as Captain Berger had ordered Christine to do when she led him to the door.

On their way to the Alperts they passed a group of American soldiers standing under the street sign *Adolf Hitler-Strasse.* They were holding a swastika flag between them, grimacing into the camera of one of their comrades. Mother suddenly remembered that she had forgotten to destroy the school flag. She was sure the Americans would find it in Ulrich's room in the lower chest drawer. But she did not say anything. It was too late anyway.

When the Bachmanns returned after three days, they found the apartment door wide open. Mother entered carefully. She peeked into the kitchen and moved slowly along the hallway into the living room.

"Oh, no, no!" she screamed, throwing her arms up. "Look, what they have done!"

The children pressed from behind. Furniture had been turned over and thrown about. Food left-overs were all over the floor. The glass of the grandfather clock was broken, and the large swastika school flag was draped over Papa's deep brown leather chair. Mother picked up the flag and handed it to Christine. There was a swastika carved into the seat.

Mother turned pale.

"Papa's favorite chair," she whispered, tears streaming down her face as she stroked the fine leather with her right hand. "Oh my God!" She sighed.

"Put the flag in the children's room under the bed, we'll burn it tonight when we light the stove." She said.

"No, mother," Christine said. "We'll take the swastika off . . . you see, it's easy and we can use the red cloth for a skirt for Ruth."

Mother rushed to the carved oak desk that had been in the family for many generations. She began rubbing the marks from spilled drinks and grease with the palm of her hand.

"Barbarians!" she hissed.

"Soldiers—or looters?" Christine said. "The door was wide open when we came," she added.

"Harald would never do that," Mother replied, shaking her head. "He was taught to respect other people's property." She stopped rubbing and looked around.

"Take those away!" she ordered, pointing at two glasses on top of the high gloss piano. Christine picked up the glasses, filled half-way with a brownish, foul-smelling liquid. Mother brought a bottle of cleaning fluid and rags from the hall closet. She rubbed the spots on the desk again and again, as if that was all that mattered in the world now.

Ruth called from the storage room by the kitchen.

"Look at this! You won't believe this! They have eaten all the pears and plums and smashed the jars on the floor. Oh, God, there is glass all over this place."

"Stay where you are!" Christine urged, covering the leather chair with a blanket from the bedroom. "I'll be right there."

"Ulrich, get a broom and sweep the floors, then get a bucket with water and get down on your hands and knees and wash them well," Christine ordered. "We have to get rid of the smell before it sinks into the furniture."

She rushed to the storage room to help Ruth out of the broken glass.

"Gerhard, take Manfred to the big bed and play with him while we are cleaning up this mess!"

An instance later, Christine called from the storage room:

"Everybody come here and see what I have found. But stay by the door, there's too much glass on the floor!" She held up a large silver coin.

"Let me see! Let me hold it! It's real silver! That's real American money!" They passed it from hand to hand.

"It's an American dollar," Christine said. "And here it says" 'In God We Trust.' They, too, trust in God, just like we. It must be hard for God sometimes to decide what to do. And look at that eagle! This is going to be my Good Luck piece for the future." She dropped it into her apron pocket.

"But it's a real dollar. It's foreign money. You have to turn that in, Christine. Otherwise you'll go to jail." Ulrich said.

"But this can be our family secret."

"Then it belongs to the family. Why should you have it?" Ulrich had stepped into the storage room to look for more coins.

"Because I found it," Christine retorted. "And, after all, I am cleaning up this awful mess. Now—everybody get out and away from the broken glass!"

The boys went back to the living room. Ulrich started to clean up, picking up food remnants from furniture and window sills.

"Christine, come here!" he called out. "Look who's here, the bread man."

"The bread man, the bread man . . ." The younger children rushed to the window and waved to the soldier.

"Pick me up . . . pick me up!" Manfred stretched his arms up to Ulrich. Christine looked through the drawn curtains of the other window. There, on his helmet, sat the American soldier who had given them the bread. Ulrich had lifted Manfred on his shoulders. He took his hand and made him wave at the soldier. The soldier smiled and continued to look up.

"He's a military policeman," Ulrich said. "I want to go down and talk to him."

"Everybody get away from the window and back to work!" Mother ordered. Ulrich took Manfred back to the bedroom and lowered him onto the bed to join Gerhard, who was playing with his tin soldiers. He went to his closet to get a sweater.

Oh, no!" he shouted. "They have taken my accordion, Christine," he said, his eyes filling with tears. "It's gone from the closet."

"I don't believe it! I can't believe that the Americans have taken your accordion," Christine said. "But don't tell Mother, she is upset enough."

Ulrich vented his anger and frustration by vigorously attacking the floor.

In the evening, when the apartment was clean, the family sat around the kitchen table, eating tired boiled potatoes which they dipped in oil and flavored with salt.

Hitler's 56th birthday on April 20 went almost unnoticed. For hours there was no electricity, and when it was on, the radio emitted music. At the end of the month numerous rumors about Hitler's death surfaced, brought in by refugees coming from the east.

"He died at the head of his troops defending Berlin," some insisted. "He died during a bombing raid and his friends burned his body right away so it would not fall into enemy hands," said others. "No, that was a German soldier they burned!" "He isn't dead. He's sitting in his mountain fortress in Bavaria watching us rot away in the mess he created." "He killed himself with his true love Eva Braun." "The *Fuhrer*—romantic?" "Yes, it was Hitler they burned in the courtyard of the Reich Chancellery. Some people have sworn to it!" "No, someone saw him fleeing with Bormann." "Let's face it, he's been dead for a while, when was the last time he spoke to us?" "No, it really was the *Fuhrer* they found in that courtyard. They could tell by the teeth!" And on and on it went.

Most people in Bahrenberg did not care whether Hitler was alive or dead. If he was dead, fine. If he got away, nobody could do anything about it. It was only normal that those most guilty of crimes had found a safe haven long before the end of the war.

"Who cares?" people would say, shrugging their shoulders. "Leave us alone! We have our own lives to get together again. We've had enough!"

Christine saw Mother looking at the postcard she had kept, the one that showed Magda Goebbels with her five young children.

"Imagine!" she sighed. "She poisoned them all."

Chapter 5

Six weeks had passed since the arrival of the Americans. It was an extraordinary spring, sunny and warm. Few Germans took notice of the weather. They were busy starting a new life. Most people left their homes only to search for food and gather information from the bulletin board, the only source for news and instructions. They still feared reprisals from former slave laborers. But when US military police, the MPs, began patrolling the streets on a regular schedule, always in twos and sometimes with a young Pole in their midst as their "helper," more people ventured out into the streets.

Ulrich and Gerhard spent most of their time around the Americans trying to get food. They never brought anything home, but talked about the "nice American soldiers who gave them things." The food stores were empty. Whenever possible, one family member stood in line, only to find that the sugar was gone, or the butter. There was no meat, no fresh fruit, no vegetables, and often no salt. But the people remained calm, they understood, at least one did not have to worry about attacks from low flying planes while standing in line for food.

For the past days the school rooms had been readied as shelters where refugees could stay during curfew hours or for a few days until they could continue their journey towards the west. The people of Bahrenberg hoped that all refugees would move on and not become a burden on the already insufficient food supply. Yet some stayed, registered for ration cards, and were housed in the dwellings vacated by former slave laborers. Most of them, even though tired from traveling on foot for months, left within a few days, insisting that the Russians would come to Bahrenberg soon.

"The Americans don't give up what they have conquered," a local man said.

"But they are Allies, they share, they are friends."

"Allies, yes—friends, no. How can they be? They have nothing in common. They are opposites in their ideologies."

"Yes," an old man said, stroking his beard. "The Americans are making a big mistake. They should take the rest of the German army, put the prisoners of war in uniform, and drive the Russians back to Moscow, or there'll be another war."

"No, there will be no more wars," a woman said. "The whole world has seen what war is like. All of Europe is destroyed. And the Russians and Americans, too, had to bury many of their young. Such a waste! No, no one can rejoice at the end of a war."

"That was truly a historic moment when the two world powers shook hands at Torgau on the Elbe. No, there will be no more wars."

Christine and Mother were washing the living room windows with a mixture of water and vinegar as the first refugees were moved into the downstairs classrooms. They saw three men and a woman entering the house of their neighbor Becker across the street. The group left the door wide open. There were loud arguments and the sound of falling furniture. They returned, their arms loaded with bed linens and clothing, and started running down *Adolf-Hitler-Strasse.*

Shots rang out—screams—shouts. The sound of running boots on the cobblestones! More shots, the smell of fired guns. People ran for cover. Some threw themselves flat on the street, covering their heads with their arms. The group dropped their loads and disappeared in the alley leading to the laborers' quarters. One man reappeared and tried to pick up some of the sheets. A lone shot, the man fell to the ground, lifeless. Several women who had been caught in the fire, got up. An MP ordered them to pick up the linens and follow him to the Becker's house. The entered the house together. The MPs asked Mr. Becker:

"Are these yours?"

Mr. Becker nodded.

"Put those on the table over there!" The MP ordered the women, and, pointing to the door he shouted:

"Now—get out!"

Christine and Mother went downstairs to see if they could help in any way.

The classroom was filled with old men, women and children, huddling on the floor. The women were dressed in the traditional East Prussian multi-layered dark skirts, which they spread out for the children to sit on. The penetrating odor of unwashed bodies and clothes mingled with the stench of urine and smell of onions and cabbage.

A scream chilled the air. All eyes turned to an older woman. Her small, deeply wrinkled face was almost completely covered by a black shawl. Her layered skirt was folded back, showing long military underwear. Her felt boots, from which pieces of rags protruded, looked enormous.

"God's wrath is upon us," she screamed, throwing her arms up and bending the upper half of her body backwards in a contorted posture. A young woman rushed towards her, covering the woman's mouth with her hands to stop the eerie screaming. But the old woman was strong and dealt heavy blows to anyone who came near her. Finally, exhausted, she fell to the floor and immediately began to snore.

"We cannot help these people and we will stay away from them," Mother told Christine. "Just think of all the diseases they might carry. The Americans are here. They'll take care of them; and they'll help us all to have a normal life someday."

"I talked to Ben Parnell today," Ulrich said during the evening meal. "He wants to meet you, Christine."

"Who is Ben Parnell?" Mother's voice showed suspicion. She continued to ladle the thin cabbage soup into the soup plates.

"The bread man, Ben . . . the MP . . . our soldier," Ulrich replied. "He asked what your name was. He thinks Christine is a nice name, says they have girls by the name of Christine in America, too. He showed me his ID card. It says his home is in Washington, but he says he is really from Arlington, Virginia. He asked how old you are. I told him you are eighteen. He says he wants to talk to you—and . . ." Ulrich moved his head from side to side, grinning. "He thinks you are very pretty."

Ruth und Gerhard giggled.

"Why did you say she's eighteen?" Mother asked annoyed.

"It sounds more grown-up. He liked it, he smiled." Christine continued to eat her soup in silence.

"And you should do something about your dumb braids," Ulrich continued. "They make you look too young."

He got up and strutted around the kitchen, hands in his pockets, proud of his knowledge of men-women relationships.

"All you need is a cigarette in your mouth, and the fool is complete," Christine snapped. She knew he had been smoking, she had found cigarette butts in his trouser pockets several times.

"Why not?" Ulrich quipped. "I am a man now. If I can work, I can smoke."

"Christine will not talk to the American soldiers," Mother said quietly. "What will people think? And our prisoners of war . . . have you forgotten what we went through, the bombings and all? And Papa and Harald! God only knows where they are, probably being beaten up in one of their POW camps."

"If the Americans have them, they are lucky," Ulrich said. "The Americans don't beat their prisoners . . . and you should see what they eat. The prisoners get the same stuff their own soldiers get. Just look at the POWs, they are all happy and smiles. Turning to Christine, he added:

"We should be nice to the Americans, especially you, Christine. Maybe they'll give us something to eat . . . and cigarettes . . .

"...and chocolate and gum," Ruth chirped.

Mother watched Christine placing the plates into the sink, and said:

"Christine will stay away from the American soldiers."

Turning to the younger children, she added:

"Get your things ready for the night. In ten minutes the electricity will be off again."

The sound of drums and loud music brought the Bachmanns to the living room windows on Sunday morning. A large procession, surrounded by American military police and villagers, mostly children, moved along *Breite Strasse* toward the church. Four wedding couples, next to each other, walked solemnly behind a band of four, two men with accordions, one with a trumpet, and one with a huge drum. The women wore white dresses and bridal veils, the men dark suits with a white flower, made from tulle, in their lapels. Three little girls in starched white dresses, large white bows in their long open hair, skipped in front of the couples, dropping young leaves and flower petals into the couples' path. The band stepped briefly aside as several people took pictures.

"Poles are getting married," Mother said, leaning out of the window to get a better look at the approaching wave of people. "It looks like finally Poles and Germans are at peace with each other," she added.

Christine rushed to the window. Shading her eyes from the bright sun, she said:

"Is Jovanka one of the brides?"

Christine had known Jovanka for more than two years. During the summer vacation in 1943 all school children had to help in the sugar beet fields. Christine had always fallen behind in separating the young plants. From the second day on this young Polish girl had taken the row next to Christine and had quickly crossed over to help Christine catch up. About a year ago, in a secret place, Jovanka had shown Christine the white lace her mother had sent from Poland for Jovanka's wedding dress. And she had told Christine that the Nazi Government had refused permission for her and Vladislav, whom she had met soon after her arrival in Bahrenberg, to get married.

"We'll just have to wait until the war is over," Jovanka had said with a sad smile, "if then we are still alive."

Yes, Jovanka was one of the brides. Her day had finally come.

Ulrich had rushed downstairs at the first sound of the music and now came running up.

"They have my accordion," he shouted. "The Poles have my accordion. Watch when they come closer. I must talk to the military police. I know it's mine. Look! The red one, that's mine."

The whole family watched nervously from the window.

"Yes, Ulrich, that's yours," Christine said. "There is only one red one in this village."

"I think he lives in the Kohler's laborer apartments," Ulrich said. "I'll run down and get the military police while they are still in the street." He ran from one window to the other.

"Not now, Ulrich!" Christine grabbed Ulrich who was just about to leave the room. "I promise I'll take care of this as soon as this wedding is over. We are not going to spoil Jovanka's wedding."

She returned to the window and waved and shouted:

"Jovaaankaaa . . . !" And the petit girl, her long black braids fastened around her head like a crown, from which a soft white veil enveloped her whole figure, waved shyly back with her small bouquet of spring flowers.

Ulrich, his whole body vibrating from anger, looked once more down at the crowd and then stomped to his room.

On her way to the bulletin board the next morning, Christine saw Ben Parnell and his co-patrol coming down *Breite Strasse. I'll ask him, I promised Ulrich. No, I can't. Yes, I must.* She started to blush. *Oh, God, what will he think when I walk up to him like this?* She walked slower, trying to control herself. *I'll ask him tomorrow. No, I must do it today, Ulrich is waiting.*

The two soldiers, unaware of Christine's inner turmoil, smiled as they walked in soldierly step in the middle of the cobblestone street.

"Excuse me," Christine said, walking toward them. Trying to control her nervousness, she told them about the accordion.

"Do you know where it is?" asked Ben.

"It's probably in that house," Christine said, pointing to the laborer cottage across the street.

"Let's go in and get it, Russ!" Ben turned to his co-patrol. Turning back to Christine, he said:

"You should come with us. You know what it looks like."

Together they walked to the three-story building. Several young women sat on wooden chairs outside the entrance, taking in the spring sun. Men were milling by the door and in the downstairs hallway. Several sat on the stairs, smoking Lucky Strikes from a package lying on the steps.

"We came to talk to the man with the accordion," Ben said.

"I play an accordion," one of the men in his forties said.

"Can we see it?" Ben asked.

"Certainly . . . Sir," the man said, performing a mock bow and walking towards the back of the hallway. The other men laughed.

The three waited. It seemed an eternity. The men were laughing and chatting. Christine felt uncomfortable. Finally, the man appeared with a black accordion.

"Is this the one you want to see?" he said, grinning.

"No, we are looking for a red one that belongs to this young lady," Russ said.

"Oh, is THAT so?" the man sneered, his mouth smiling, his eyes furious. "It seems to me, ah . . . gentlemen . . . ah you came to the wrong place. There is no red accordion here." Still in a mocking tone he added:

"But, of course, you gentlemen are free to search this place. However," he took a deep breath, stretching himself, "we think it is a waste of time." He bowed again, and again the others laughed.

All Christine wanted was to get out. She was embarrassed and angry. The two MPs walked behind her as they crossed the street. The group stopped for a moment.

"I am really sorry," Christine said, her voice shaking. She wanted to say how bad she felt for having put the soldiers through such an embarrassing situation, but she was trembling too much.

"Don't worry," Ben said, trying to comfort her. "I'm just sorry we did not find it, but at least we tried.

Christine quickly shook hands with the men and hurried away as the two continued on their beat. She did not mention the incident at home.

The next afternoon, as Christine and Mother walked arm in arm along *Breite Strasse* to visit Mrs. Alpert. The man the MPs had questioned approached them with quick steps. Ignoring Mother, he grabbed Christine by the throat with both hands, pressing it tightly with his thumbs, bending her head backwards. Christine felt Mother's arm slipping from hers. She gasped for air and felt the grip tightening. *I'm dying . . . he is killing me . . . right here.*

He pressed tighter. Then, suddenly, he released the grip. Christine, choking with tears, coughed as she held her throat and neck. The man brought his face close to Christine's and hissed, his breath reeking with whiskey:

"I warn you." He grabbed her shoulders and held them in a tight grip. "If you come back one more time with an American MP to search for your accordion, or for anything else, I'll break your neck . . . I swear to God!"

He slipped away.

Mother had slumped to the ground.

"Get up, Mama!" Christine whispered under tears, trying to help Mother up. "Come on, Mama, let's go home!"

People began crowding around.

"Move on . . . move on! What's wrong?" A passing MP patrol had spotted the gathering and tried to disperse the crowd.

Christine looked up.

"Can we help? What happened?" one MP asked.

"No, thank you . . . it's alright, just a little accident. My mother, she—slipped on the curb, but she is alright now. Thank you." She took Mother's arm and slowly they started to walk.

"I checked about your accordion today," Christine told Ulrich that evening. "The man who had it went west last night."

Chapter 6

other watched from the living room as Christine and Ulrich joined other women and older children walking to their new working place. A slice of dark, heavy bread, sprinkled with sugar, and a cup of peppermint tea, was the only nourishment until they would return at night. But next Friday they would bring the first 'extra' Mr. Kohler had promised.

American guards on both sides, the German POWs marched in military formation to the Ottersberg Estate to be detailed for field labor. Their cheerful singing showed the civilians how happy they were to be under American control. For them the war was over.

Gerhard, Ruth and Manfred were still asleep. Mother moved her chair closer to the window and started to knit while watching the people in the street. Other neighbors leaned out of their windows. Hermann Bretten, who lived with his parents across the street, nodded a friendly "good morning" to Mother, bowing slightly in gentlemanly fashion. Mother returned the greeting with a nod and a smile as she adjusted her sweater to protect her shoulders from the May chill. Hermann was one of the few young men who had spent the war years at home, helping his father in their prosperous construction business. He was born with a 'bad leg', as people said, and they commented on how lucky he had been to be at home all those years. God only knew how their husbands and sons would return some day, if they returned at all. Hermann always had a friendly word for anyone he chanced to meet on his frequent walks through town.

He must be twenty-eight now, Mother thought. Young girls and several war widows tried to get his attention. He would be the perfect husband with a ready-made nest for a lucky girl. The gossipers knew that he wanted to marry Christine. Once he had told her how foolish it was for her to study so hard and concentrate on learning foreign languages, when all she needed to know was how to cook, sew and bake.

"Someday you'll get married and all that studying was a waste," he had said, but Christine had just laughed and walked away.

But times had changed. Responding to Hermann's greeting, Mother wondered if Christine might not change her mind should he propose. Germany had lost the war. The future the Bachmanns had planned for their children was over. Many universities in the cities had been destroyed by bombs and fighting. It would be years before plans could be made again. By that time Christine would be too old to start anything. She should get married and have children. But since there was still no word from Papa and Harald, Christine, as the oldest one, would first have to earn a living for the family. The new administration had not made a decision if Papa's salary would continue to come, especially since his Nazi past had not been fully examined. Until fall Christine could work in the fields so they would get special food on Fridays, a great help while the stores were empty. Later Christine should learn to type and write shorthand and get a secretarial job in Schoenebeck. Marrying Hermann would greatly help.

Mother looked at the sky. An airplane, a silver spot with a long white tail, for years an ominous sign of an imminent air raid, was now a welcome symbol of protection. During the war the people had come to hate sunny days. A cloudy day usually meant no air attacks on Magdeburg.

Mother was disappointed when next Friday the children brought only a jar of sugar beet syrup.

"Mr. Kohler says that's all he can give us. He has a quota to fill. Controls have become very tight. With the refugees there are so many more people that need to be fed, after harvest time things should look better," Christine said.

On May 9 the notice of Germany's unconditional surrender appeared on the bulletin board. Already the day before the news had been announced through the bullhorn. Nothing changed in the daily life. While Christine and Ulrich worked in the fields, Mother took the younger children to the food lines, or they gathered firewood by the pond. Christine stayed in the field during the half-hour noon break, just resting or munching on dry bread and cold boiled potatoes. Separating the tiny sugar beet plants was tedious and tiring, and Christine always fell behind. During the carrot harvest she almost ate a carrot, but decided not to, she could be punished for depriving her people of essential foods.

Ulrich still visited the American soldiers when he could. One evening he handed Christine a folded note.

"It's from Ben, he is leaving for Japan," he said.

Christine opened the note. There was an address, and underneath it read: "This is my home address, please write to me when you can. Hope to see you again. Ben Parnell."

The bulk of the American troops had gradually moved out of Bahrenberg. Only forces essential to the functioning of the administration remained. When on June 15 British soldiers, together with Americans, began patrolling the streets, the people of Bahrenberg were startled. Some people tried to talk to the British soldiers, but they moved away, avoiding contact with the German population.

Christine was determined to question one of the Englishmen. One morning, going to work, she walked up to the American-British patrol coming down *Breite Strasse*. Looking straight at the British soldier, she asked:

"Do you think the Russians will come here?"

He shifted his beret with an uncomfortable gesture.

"Why are you so afraid of the Russians?" he asked. "They are not worse than your soldiers were during the war. Are the Americans as bad as your propaganda made them out to be? You see, it's the same with the Russians. German propaganda made everybody look bad. Just to scare the people and keep the soldiers fighting."

Thousands of refugees could not be lying about the killings and burnings of whole villages when the Russians came, Christine thought.

"Honestly, I really don't know," the soldier spoke again. "I don't think anyone here knows. If they come, they'll not come as fighting troop like in the east, but as peaceful occupation forces. The war is over. Order must be restored. There is really nothing to worry about."

Christine did not tell her family about the conversation. In her imagination she created monstrous situations in which she saw herself if the Russians came to Bahrenberg.

Since the Americans showed no signs of moving out, the people came to believe that the area around Magdeburg would be occupied jointly by British and American troops. Most of the refugees, however, did not want to take any chances and left for the western zones. Several adventurous young *Bahrenbergers* joined them, feeling they had nothing to lose and perhaps much to gain by leaving Bahrenberg.

Chapter 7

On Sunday, July 1, 1945, at 2:00 in the morning, the Russians arrived in Bahrenberg. The wail of a siren tore the stillness of the night. The Bachmanns jumped from their beds and rushed to the windows without turning on the lights.

"*Achtung! Achtung!*" An announcer shouted from a jeep in a German with a strong Russian accent.

"Effective immediately this town is under the control of the Soviet Occupation Forces."

"We are trapped! We should have gone west!" Christine shouted.

"Everybody get dressed!" Mother said.

As the jeep drove down *Breite Strasse*, the Bachmanns could hear fragments of sentences like "instructions—not permitted to leave the homes—curfew—further instructions to follow in the morning." And then, again, closer: "Resistance and refusal to obey orders will be punished by death."

In a silence heavy with shock and disbelief the Bachmanns watched as the new masters drove around Bahrenberg several times. The speaker insisted that the Russians had not come as conquerors. The enemy, Hitler's Germany, was now destroyed. Germans and Russians, as friends and brothers, must now work together to build a Germany free from Fascism and militarism. No one must be afraid.

"We are stuck," Christine said. "It is now too late to leave."

"We had no choice," Mother replied. "How would Papa and Harald find us? With no mail we couldn't even write to anyone telling them of our whereabouts."

She peeked through the curtains. Turning to Christine, she continued:

"This is our home. This and our family is all we have, and it is more than thousands of other people have now. I just couldn't leave everything behind and walk with a few suitcases into an unknown future." Again she looked out of the window, adding:

"They can't be all that bad."

The family waited by the windows for the truckloads of soldiers that would occupy Bahrenberg, but they did not come. Only a few black civilian cars sped towards the Ottersberg Estate. They sat by the large entrance, leaving their headlights on, then some drove out the back road.

The rumbling of military vehicles behind the Ottersberg Estate could be heard for hours. In the darkness of the night the shouting of military orders signaled to the people that a new era had begun for Bahrenberg.

Mother and Christine continued to watch from the living room window. The younger children had, one by one, drifted back to bed, exhausted from being up most of the night.

In the morning, shortly after 8 o'clock, a little two-wheeled square wooden wagon, drawn by a small shaggy horse, drove around the corner by the church. A stocky Russian in military uniform with large gold-colored shoulder bars, sitting on a heap of straw, was waving with both arms, a bottle in one hand. Making shrieking noises, he looked left and right, waving constantly.

"Look at this!" Christine cried out. "These are the people who won the war. What ever happened? Where did Germany go wrong? We had the best soldiers in the world. How was it ever possible?"

The cart sped towards the Ottersberg Estate and disappeared in the main entrance.

"They might not even bother bringing troops here," Mother said. "The rumbling last night, they probably went right on to Magdeburg. I think they just occupy the big cities, and we'll get just a few for administrative purposes, as with the Americans."

About an hour after the arrival of the horse-drawn wagon, an American jeep drove along Breite Strasse.

"*Achtung! Achtung*! This territory is now officially under the control of the Soviet forces. The American troops will vacate this town by noon today," the American announcer shouted through the bullhorn.

"All German POWs under American control will be taken west. The trucks will begin loading at 10:00am. All displaced persons and refugees not yet registered in Bahrenberg are also free to leave at this time."

"You must go with them, Christine," Mother said, rushing to the bedroom to prepare a bundle for Christine.

"But how can I? Everyone knows me."

"I'll make a refugee out of you." Mother started to dress Christine in an old sweater and threw a shawl around her head.

"No, I can't—I just can't," Christine shook her head, her eyes filling with tears, her voice breaking. "I can't leave you like this, I would always worry."

"I order you to go!" Mother said in a determined voice. "Stop it! We have little time. You are young, and no matter how strict the controls, the Russian soldiers are barbarians. They cannot change overnight. No, I won't have it. I would never forgive myself if something happened to you here. You will go!"

"Go, Christine!" Ulrich urged. "I'll take care of Mother. And after you get settled in the West, you'll get us all across. By then Papa and Harald should be home."

"We should all go," Christine tried one more time. "We have one more chance."

Without another word, Mother pushed Christine out of the door. She never had a chance to say goodbye to the younger children. At the last moment Mother had pressed a small bundle with Christine's best clothes and a few slices of bread and cold boiled potatoes into her hands, embraced her quickly and said:

"Tomorrow you will find work in the west. Go to the farmers, they can feed you. And if the people ask you if you can do this or that, never say no, always say yes, I can do it."

Mother gave Christine a light push and closed the door.

Christine watched as the German prisoners-of-war were led to the American trucks. Since most of the refugees that wanted to go west had already left, there would be enough room for anyone wanting to leave. Two other Bahrenberg girls, disguised like Christine, were waiting for their space. No one spoke.

Christine turned back to look at her home. She saw Ulrich and Mother watching the proceedings. She started to walk back, but Mother pulled Ulrich into the doorway and they disappeared. A deep loneliness overcame Christine. She was still unsure whether she was doing the right thing.

An MP walked along the trucks.

"Whoever is going, get on the trucks—now! Everybody else get back! The trucks are about to move out!" he shouted.

Several Russian soldiers were watching the evacuation from a few meters away.

"Come on, little doll!" A German POW called from one of the trucks. The back flap of the truck was down. The soldiers made room for Christine. She threw her bundle up and stretched her arms out. Two POWs helped her up and settled her between them on the edge.

The American MP motioned to the driver that the truck was ready to leave. The driver started the motor with a loud noise. A big wave of fumes enveloped the riders. As the truck began to move, Christine looked once more for her family, but they were gone. The truck moved slowly, trying to get in line with the other vehicles leaving Bahrenberg on the only major road toward the highway Halberstadt-Magdeburg. Many American soldiers threw chocolates and gum to the children who had gathered by the roadside to wave a last goodbye.

The convoy had just crossed the railroad tracks. The burned-out railroad car was still on the tracks; a reminder of that tragic day in April. Christine thought about that day, when the Americans had come to Bahrenberg, and how, for the first time in years she had dared to think of a new life. Now they were on their way out, and she was going with them to the west into a promising future. But her family—she could not finish the thought. Her heart was pounding. Mother was still young, and Ruth almost thirteen, and the little ones . . . would she ever see them again? Every day she would worry. Her mind screamed, *'no, I can't—I can't do it. Yes, I must, Mother wants me to, no—yes—Mother—no—yes—No!*

"Stop!" she screamed, "stop! I want to get off—I don't want to go, I can't—stop!"

She tried to jump off the truck. The POWs grabbed her arms.

"Don't be foolish," they shouted, tightening the grip. "You'll get hurt."

"Let me go! Let me go!" she screamed as loud as she could.

The driver had heard the noise and was now looking back, slowing down as he did. The following truck widened the gap between the two trucks when the driver noticed the struggle.

Christine jumped onto the pavement, falling backwards. She scrambled to her feet and ran between the houses toward the alley by the church. She climbed over the wall surrounding the church, ran through the cemetery along the gravel path past big graves, jumping over smaller ones, out the main entrance, towards home. She never looked back.

Mother was standing by the kitchen table, cutting up sheets to be used as towels. She looked up when Christine opened the apartment door. Without a word she continued to cut.

Christine, still shaken, her eyes filled with tears, went to the living room where the younger children were playing cards on the floor. They smiled at her briefly before continuing their game. Christine wondered if Mother had even told them that she had been on the way to the west. She walked to the bedroom to change her clothes. Only then did she realize that the few nice clothes she had owned had gone west.

Ulrich walked into the living room as Christine was coming from the bedroom. He looked at her but did not say anything when he saw how upset she was.

"Perhaps it is better after all that we are together," Mother said in a calm voice later. "But remember, you did have a choice—a chance."

The incident was never mentioned again.

More Soviet troops arrived in the afternoon. First came two black sedans, driven by soldiers. Through the open window one could see three officers in the first car, two civilians and an officer in the second car. Two middle-sized trucks with about 30 soldiers each followed. The soldiers were standing, pointing their weapons at the houses. Most people were looking through their curtains. The streets were empty except for a few old men, who were smiling at the soldiers, waving red flags from which the swastika had been removed, the circle still visible. Again the loudspeaker came around, telling the people not to be afraid, but to stay indoors until further notice later in the day. All able-bodied persons must appear at their working place the next morning so work in the fields would not be delayed. The local government, established by the Americans, would remain in effect. Changes would be announced on the bulletin board or through the loudspeaker. Attacks on members of the occupation forces would be punished by death.

The next morning Christine and Ulrich returned to the Kohlers to continue working in the fields. The feeling of relaxation and comfort the villagers of Bahrenberg had enjoyed for three months had left with the Americans the day before. Fear and apprehension had replaced it, but for most Germans, who had lived under an oppressive regime for so many years that it had become a normal situation, the change was not drastic. They had not had time to shake their suspicious and fearful lifestyle acquired during Nazi times. The new situation seemed almost normal, something they had been used to.

That afternoon Mayor Krieger was seen walking to the Ottersberg Estate, in his best suit, wearing a red shirt that his spouse had sewn for him overnight from two Nazi flags. She had carefully avoided showing the round markings where the swastika had been.

Chapter 8

Life in Bahrenberg had changed overnight. The streets were deserted again. People spoke in whispers and tried to avoid attention. The young women and girls who had begun to blossom under the admiring eyes of the American soldiers, went back to their drab clothes, trying to look old and ugly. For several days the loudspeaker urged the people to relax and not be afraid. Again and again the speaker stressed that the Red Army had come as a peaceful occupation force, as friends and brothers. It had come to help the German people to rout out Fascism, to rebuild Germany. Yet, the people were afraid.

There was no violence. On the surface the atmosphere was calm. Still, there was a strong undercurrent of fearful insecurity, of distrust, a feeling that something might happen anytime, anywhere, like in the shadow of a dormant volcano. The Russian soldiers patrolling the streets were tense, quick to ready their guns when communicating with adults. They, too, were suspicious. But they loved the children.

As the weeks passed, people gradually moved around more freely. On Sundays, little girls showed off their new red dresses made from swastika flags, and their white knee socks knit in a cable stitch pattern from the cotton yarn their mothers had picked up at the train in April. There were no red skirts in the Bachmann family. Before the Russians arrived, Mother had quietly dropped their swastika flag into the village pond on one of her walks to collect firewood.

In the morning the local train took the workers to Schoenebeck and Magdeburg. Only people with a valid pass could board the train. More and more it seemed that the Russians were there to stay. In the beginning, information about the borders between the East and West Zones changed daily. Weeks later it was confirmed that the border between the Russian Zone on one side, and the American and British Zones on the other, would run near Helmstedt, further south through the Harz mountains, and in the north near Rebenau, in the District of Wiedenbeck, where Christine's maternal grandparents lived.

New registrations were announced. People were warned to be absolutely honest about their past. The new administration was "determined to wipe out Fascism which had caused so much bloodshed and destruction throughout Europe."

During the registration the new masters discovered that more than fifty adults of those registered in April did not show up. Two days before the Russians arrived, Count Bodo von Ottersberg, who had lived in a part of his estate while the Americans were occupying his house, had also left for the west with two horse-drawn wagons.

"I don't know why he left," Luise, his servant for many years, sobbed at the registration. "He hated the Nazis. He was a good man if I ever saw one, a real gentleman."

The Ottersberg Estate became, once again, the headquarters, this time of the *Kommandantura*.

The Bachmann family was gathering in the living room when, one evening, they heard a light knock on the door. Manfred jumped up and ran out before the others had heard it. He opened the door, peeked out, slammed it shut and ran back into the living room.

"There's a beggar at the door, maybe a soldier. I think a he wants some bread," he said, excitement in his voice.

"I told you not to open the door," Mother admonished him, while going out to see for herself.

She stared at the soldier in his torn military coat. She searched the piercing eyes and began to tremble.

"Harald!" she whispered. Harald!" They rushed into each other's arms, unable to speak. Mother felt the skeleton figure under the ragged uniform.

"Harald—my God, what have they done to you?" She held him again, afraid he would disappear if she let go of him. "My God, I—I-you're home!"

The siblings were now standing silently by the living room door, instinctively aware that this moment belonged to Mother and Harald.

"Have you heard from Papa?" Harald asked.

Mother shook her head and closed the door. Now the group came alive. One by one they rushed forward throwing their arms around their big brother.

"You look funny when you smile," Manfred piped with embarrassment, "like if you're crying."

"You must be hungry," Mother said, leading him to the sofa. She rushed to the kitchen, taking Harald's torn canvas bag with her. Brothers and sisters crowded around Harald, spilling out anything they could think of in the excitement.

Christine looked at her brother. At seventeen, less than a year ago, he had left home to fight the enemy. He had been so proud and handsome in his new uniform. At eighteen he had returned an old man.

Harald began to remove his coat, seemingly with great effort. Gerhard rushed forward to help him.

"Handle it gently," Harald joked. "It's the only one I have."

Returning from the kitchen, Mother placed a slice of bread and a cup of chamomile tea before Harald.

Soon your old clothes will fit you again," she said, arranging the embroidered cushions on the sofa so Harald would be more comfortable. Manfred sat next to his big brother and held his hand.

Harald was too tired to talk, and, soon after eating the meager meal, got up and went to bed.

A few days later, during registration, Harald met Mr. Otto Hildebrand, who welcomed him home and handed him, together with his ration cards, an application for teacher training.

"We need new and young teachers to replace the old Nazi-indoctrinated ones as quickly as possible. Your training will begin soon." He turned back to the man gathering the ration cards and said:

"Make that a few extras, Paul, he must regain his strength, he is a new teacher."

Chapter 9

The reopening of the schools inspired new hope for Christine. She was tired of working in the fields under the suspicious eyes of the foreman, with Russian soldiers guarding the German prisoners-of-war they had brought in. The take-home portions on Fridays were not worth mentioning. There were rumors that the food situation would get worse, for the Russian forces must be supported by the German economy. Negotiations were under way that the four occupation powers were planning that the eastern part, largely an agricultural area, would have to help the west. Eating a carrot during harvest time had now become an act of sabotage.

Christine, her face dirty with dusty sweat and smelling of onions, removed her kerchief and sat down on the kitchen bench. Harald told her that the schools might now open in September, on time.

"Are you sure, Harald?" she beamed. "I can't believe it! I wonder which ones of my teachers will come back."

"You'd better rid yourself of that grime and smell. It might grow into your skin and you'll keep it for life," Harald teased. "An educated lady smelling of onions is hardly attractive."

Christine walked to the kitchen sink. She dipped her arms to the elbows into the cold water, splashed her face and dried it with a small washcloth hanging on a hook above the sink.

"I hate harvesting onions," she said, returning to the kitchen table. "I've had a headache all day and my eyes haven't stopped burning."

"Someone else will have to harvest the potatoes and sugar beets in the fall," Harald said, trying to cheer her up.

A few days later Harald traveled to Magdeburg to attend his first training session for new teachers. In the evening he told Christine that her school, the *Luisenschule*, had been destroyed during a bombing raid on Magdeburg. This meant that a new alternative for Christine's education must be found. Mother suggested that Christine should enter a vocational school in Schoenebeck, learn typing and shorthand. She should take one of the Russian language courses that would, undoubtedly, spring up everywhere. She must also improve her English and French language skills and her wish to become an interpreter would soon come true. But Harald felt that, since Christine had less than a year to graduation, she should complete her high school education. Without a graduation certificate she would never be able to register for university courses. After lengthy discussions Harald, Mother, and Christine decided that it would be best to ask Oma Anna and Grandfather in the north, in Rebenau, if she could live with them for a while. From there she could attend her former high school in Wiedenbeck for the remaining semesters. A phone call was placed from the mayor's office to the mayor in Rebenau to contact the grandparents. A few days later the answer came, the grandparents would welcome her. Harald began to inquire about the necessary travel permits.

One day two big trailers, drawn by four horses each, moved slowly along Breite Strasse. The people watched and wondered what they might contain. The wagon drove to the lawn by the Ottersberg Estate, where steel bars and canvas tarps were unloaded. By Saturday a merry-go-round and a tent for dancing had been erected. Late Saturday afternoon the sounds of "I love you truly, truly, dear . . ." and "Oh Marie . . . oh, Marie . . ." came blaring over the loudspeaker and attracted the villagers. Soon the children rode around on the mechanical horses, laughing and screaming with delight. The first post-war Saturday night dance was announced over the loudspeaker and on the bulletin board.

"I'd like to go to the dance," Christine said.

"None of you is going," Mother said. "I won't have it. This is a time for mourning. I can't see why anyone would enjoy dancing on the graves of our fallen soldiers."

There was a long silence.

"I think it will be good for all of us to get away from the mourning for a while," Harald said. "It is time we learn how to live, for as long as I can remember our lives have been filled with fear, tension, and depression. We have survived the war, fortunately. We have another chance to live, really live."

"Dancing so soon after the war is—is—disrespectful, it's—immoral," Mother insisted. She got up, dropped her mending into the basket and left the room, deeply hurt.

Harald waited for a week, out of respect for Mother, but the next Saturday afternoon he took the younger children to the merry-go-round. While Ruth, Gerhard and Manfred were riding around on the horses, Harald, Christine and Ulrich were watching the dancing pairs from the entrance of the tent. Three Russian soldiers watched briefly, then ambled back to the Ottersberg Estate. Women danced with women. Children tried their first dancing steps to the tunes of a Glenn Miller record. And then again: "I love you truly . . . truly, dear," alternating with the tango "Star of Rio" and "When the Red Sun goes down over Capri . . ." A few old men stood in the corner, watching the women sway to the music, singing and humming while dancing. Soon almost the whole village either danced or stood around the dance floor. Interrupting the music, the announcer asked for anyone who can play an instrument or wanting to play in his band to come forward. A few young men walked up to the podium while the band finished the song.

"Let's go home!" Harald suggested. The three stepped outside and crossed the lawn towards the merry-go round to get the other children. All three were sitting in the grass. Manfred was crying, holding his head and stomach.

Christine bent down to console Manfred.

"You are not leaving yet, I hope?" Hermann Bretten was limping towards them at a quick pace, his face flushed. He smiled briefly at Harald and turned to Christine, watching every moment of her slight body.

"We can't stay," Harald said curtly.

"Oh, I am sorry. I was hoping to have a dance with you, Christine." He smiled embarrassed. "But if you . . . I mean, could I talk to you for a moment?"

Harald moved a few steps away.

"Not really, can't you see that Manfred is not feeling well?" Turning to Harald, she said:

"I think he stayed on the merry-go-round too long, we'd better go home."

"Just one thing," Hermann spoke again. "I just wanted to let you know, the town council will soon open a new *Konsum* store at the end of *Breite Strasse*, near the church, and I'll be the manager." He seemed to wait for a response that did not come.

"I'll visit you next week and tell you all about it, and . . . tell your mother I have something to discuss with her."

Hermann looked at Christine in a way that made her feel most uncomfortable. He briefly shook Harald's hand, still looking at Christine.

"I'll see you soon, Christine," Hermann said, bowing briefly before hurrying back to the entrance of the tent.

Christine brought Manfred to his feet and brushed the grass off his clothes. Harald picked Manfred up and lifted him onto his shoulders.

"Now you are taller than anyone around," Harald tried to cheer up his little brother.

"Let's see who gets home first!" Gerhard triggered a race among the children. Christine and Harald walked side by side.

"Christine . . . Christine . . . wait a minute! I want to talk to you."

Christine and Harald turned around. Hermann Bretten was hobbling after them, waving his arms.

"Oh, God, what does he want NOW?" Christine mumbled, disgust in her voice.

"See what he wants, Christine," Harald said. "And be careful. He has friends at the top and can make trouble for us if he wants to. I'll walk slowly ahead."

Christine strode towards Hermann who had sat down on a tree stump, wiping his forehead with a monogrammed handkerchief. He smiled at her. He jumped up and extended his pudgy white hands.

"Christine," he whispered. "You know what I was talking about before. I've loved you for a long time. I cannot keep my eyes off you. I want you for my wife. I want you to be the mother of my children!"

He tried to grasp her hands. Christine stepped back, placing her hands behind her back.

"I know you are still young," Hermann continued. "All this might be too sudden for you, but I promise you, I'll be the best husband. If you marry me, you'll never be poor again. I know where to get silk and pearls and furs, and . . ."

"I am not poor," Christine interrupted. She watched his eyes travel down her faded homespun skirt to her feet. "I just don't like wearing shoes."

She swung around and stalked away to join Harald and Manfred. Hermann followed them at a distance and disappeared in the large courtyard gate of his home.

"I want to go north," Christine said as they were walking on. "I hate getting stuck in this God-forsaken town."

Harald nodded.

"I'll talk to Mr. Alpert to start the paper work. I'll take care of Mother and the family. I am sure Papa will be home soon.

A pot of steaming boiled potatoes stood on the kitchen stove. The table was set. Mother was pouring small amounts of oil into each plate and added finely cut onions and salt. She transferred the potatoes to a large bowl and placed it in the center of the table. Manfred quickly slid to his place on the kitchen bench.

"You forgot to wash your hands," Mother said.

"But they aren't dirty," Manfred protested, turning them inside out and looking at them. He slowly made his way to the sink and slid back into his seat. All but Harald were already sitting.

" . . . anything wrong?" Mother asked, watching Harald as he washed his hands again and again.

"No lather at all," he answered. "No matter how often you wash, no lather, why's that?"

Because it's pure clay," Mother replied. "There's not a speck of fat in that soap. It's been like that for years. Just once I'd like to wash myself with the kind of soap Uncle Herbert sent from Paris when he was stationed there. That was some soap, pink and soft!" She drew a deep breath to inhale the imaginary fragrance.

Harald sat down next to Manfred who struggled with peeling a potato. Manfred smiled as he stuck his fork into a large piece and dipped it in the oil mixture. He nibbled around it until the oil was gone and coated it once more. Only the sound of the forks on the plates interrupted the silence.

"I haven't heard you playing the piano since I've come home, Christine, have you forgotten how?" Harald teased Christine after supper.

Without a word Christine sat down on the piano chair, a rectangle stool with a needlepoint cover of red roses on a background of a variety of greens. She struggled with the "Minuet in G" by Ludwig van Beethoven. When she had finished, Harald, who had been listening intently from Papa's large leather chair that was now permanently covered with a blanket, walked over to her.

"Nice, but a little heavy," he said. "When you get up north, look up your old piano teacher, what was her name, Mrs.

Martin? And take lessons again. You've come so far, it will all have been a waste if you stopped now."

Mother looked up.

"When is Christine going north?"

"We have had a long talk, Mother," Harald replied. "I think it is best for Christine to leave as soon as possible. I'll see Mr. Alpert tomorrow. It's only two weeks to the first of September. She might even have to start late."

Since Mother did not speak, Harald added:

"And if things don't work out up there, she can always come back and take that typing and shorthand course in Schoenebeck."

It will work out! It must. There is no other way. Christine thought. *I can't breathe here.*

Autumn was in the air. Dark clouds moved across a gray sky and brought the first cold rain of the season. Some days Christine was already drenched when she arrived at the Kohlers. She was glad when, instead of being handed a potato sack as protection from the rain in the field, she was sent to the barn to help with the threshing. Within a few days she had learned to tie the grain bundles at the high speed necessary for the uninterrupted threshing process. Afterwards Mr. Kohler allowed her to select long pieces of straw to take home to be used to make straw shoes. In the evening she would wet the straw in the kitchen sink for about twenty minutes to soften it. Then she and Ruth would braid the damp straw into long ropes, adding new straw as necessary. They would sew the braids together with a strong thread to form a sole. From an old garment they cut strips of clothing, hemmed them and sewed them to the sole on each side near the front, crossing them and fastening the loose ends to the middle of the sole. For the back hold they fastened strips with loops to the heel part, made from a braided cord of knitting yarns and strung them through the loops. By the end of the threshing season, each of the girls had three pairs. Mother preferred the sturdier wooden clogs to the soft-soled straw shoes.

And Mrs. Kohler taught Christine to spin flax. In the beginning Christine thought she could never learn it. The wheel, moved by a foot pedal, was always faster than her hands that tried to shape the flax into a thread that would wind itself around the spool. Often the thread broke and slipped through the opening in front of the spool. Christine watched with admiration as the other women were producing a fine, even thread. She was determined not to give up. Mrs. Kohler, a big, friendly woman, never tired of helping her.

"Try not to get too much flax between your fingers, just a little, like this . . . and try to keep it even, Christine!"

She showed Christine again and again.

"Patience, Christine," she said kindly, "is one of the greatest virtues."

" . . . and another?" Christine asked.

"Courage," Mrs. Kohler said, "Patience and courage. That's what we need in life!"

Christine continued to struggle with the spinning wheel. How surprised Oma Anna will be, she thought, when I can join her on winter evenings in the spinning of sheep wool, sitting next to Grandfather on the bench by the tall green tile stove in the living room, listening to his stories of long ago.

Chapter 10

Christine's departure was only a week away. Mr. Alpert brought the approved papers and cautioned Christine to stay close to women with children during her journey. Mother worked for days and the greater part of several nights to sew a few clothes for Christine now that the trip was official: pants from the better parts of old blankets, and a windbreaker from parachute silk traded for two spools of olive drab cotton yarn. Christine could still wear the shoes Mother had bought a size larger on ration cards almost two years before, brown leather upper, now considerably faded, with cream-colored rubber soles, called "pork rind soles," because of its resemblance in color and grainy texture to the skin of hogs.

On the last evening Christine packed a few of her favorite books. Harald urged her to carry only a minimum of baggage since train communication was still interrupted in many places, and she must be prepared to walk long stretches. The younger children wrote letters and drew pictures for their grandparents. They chatted about the Christmas vacation when Christine would return with butter, sugar and flour for baking, and perhaps a goose or duck for the Christmas dinner.

It was close to midnight when Christine tucked the younger children into bed, saying goodnight and good-bye. She would be gone the next morning when they awoke.

Christine and Harald were the only special travelers on the early morning local, the workers' train. The platform at the main station in Magdeburg was crowded with people stretched out on their belongings, oblivious to the activities around them. Red Cross nurses and Catholic sisters rushed back and forth, handing out hot liquids and gathering those too weak and sick to go on. Harald and Christine walked to the farthest end of the platform and sat down on the ground, resting their backs against a concrete pole.

"The train for Stendal will leave in fifteen minutes," the station master shouted, walking along the tracks in his blue uniform and red cap. "Everybody move back from the edge!"

Harald took a cup of hot broth from a nun and handed it to Christine. The nun waited for the cup while Christine and Harald finished the liquid.

"We haven't been to church for a long time," Christine said after the nun was gone. "I felt guilty taking a drink from her."

"I haven't felt the need to go, either," Harald replied. "My God wasn't there when I needed Him most. I think I'll try it on my own for a while." He noticed the shock in Christine's eyes. Quickly he added:

"But you, Christine, you must give Him a chance! You don't know enough about life yet to make it on your own."

"Do you think Mother and Papa really believe in God and Jesus?"

"I really don't know, Christine," Harald said after a pause. "They never talked about it. They were raised as Protestants and raised us in the same way. That's the way it's done. Yes, I've heard Papa quoting from the Bible and the New Testament at times, but I really think they sent us to church because the pastor always knows who is in church and who isn't, and he comments on it. And they're probably afraid of God. They think they get punished if they don't show up in church. And they tell us we must be good because God is watching us all the time."

"A God that waves his fingers at you constantly, like 'you'd better not do this, you must do that!' is no fun to visit on Sundays. Maybe He died in the war and we'll get a new one," Christine joked.

"I wonder if Papa will still quote from the Bible when he returns, like that stuff that Jesus died for our sins. What a cruel thing for a father to do, to burden his own son like that!" Harald mused. "I wonder how much of that is really true."

"Well, I think religion is something you have to carry around with you whether you like it or not, like the shape of your body or the color of your eyes," Christine said. "Grandfather told me once you don't really have to go to church to please God. He is the voice within you. Through that he tells you what's right and what's wrong. And if you learn to listen to that voice, you are in tune with God and need not fear him. He goes with you wherever you go."

Harald nodded.

"I think we each have to find our own God to make life bearable," he said.

The crowd on the platform began to get ready to board. As the train moved slowly into the station, many young people, mostly returning German soldiers, jumped on the steps and disappeared inside. Harald grabbed Christine's battered suitcase and the carton with the books. He leaped onto the nearest steps. Christine ran alongside the train to follow him in as soon as the train would come to a halt.

The compartment was filled with soldiers and a refugee woman with two children, about six and eight years old, whom the soldiers had helped on the train. Harald gave the seat he had reserved to Christine, embraced her briefly and worked his way out against the stream of shouting people scrambling in. He waved once more as he passed the window and moved toward the exit like a fish swimming upstream.

People were crowding the compartment and the passageway. The vile scent of unwashed bodies and clothing was overpowering. The mother of the children turned pale, holding a man's handkerchief to her mouth. She leaned back and closed her eyes.

The train had traveled less than an hour when, suddenly, it came to a halt. A soldier opened the window and leaned out. Stretching his neck, he looked left and right. Quickly all the windows were open. People shouted, wondering what was wrong. Finally the conductor appeared. He announced that the engine had broken down and that it would take several hours to replace it.

"Just stay inside and wait," he suggested. "By the way, there is a freight train leaving today from the cattle loading station not quite ten kilometers to the north for those who are good on foot."

"Let's go!" the soldier said, closing the window. The other soldiers got up, grabbing their bags.

"You, too, come on!" The soldier turned to the young mother, "We'll help with the children." The mother looked up and shook her head.

"I can't," she said. "I don't feel well." The children huddled closer to her. "I'm sorry—but thank you."

Quickly the soldier turned to Christine.

"How about you, are you coming?"

She nodded and jumped up. She took the suitcase from the baggage rack, then bent down and pulled the carton by its string from underneath the seat. Instantly other passengers took the vacated spaces.

A group of about 20 young men and women walked north along the railroad tracks and followed the sign to the *Remsdorf* Life Stock Loading Station. One soldier took Christine's parcel when he saw that she was falling behind.

"What's your name?" he asked.

"Christine Bachmann."

"I'm Hans Kruppsberg. The guy . . ."

"Joachim Hans VON Kruppsberg is that gentleman's name," the soldier walking in front of them mocked. "He's a VON . . . one of our German elite from the old times . . . but I guess it doesn't really matter now. We all lost the war together."

Hans blushed and laughed embarrassed.

"Like Joachim Hans von Ziethen, the Hussar General?" Christine said, laughing.

"Well, anyway . . ." Hans continued. "What I was going to say, the big chap in front is Gustav Schiller—no relation to the great poet, though. The one to his left is Karl-Heinz Mollenhauer. Those two came from the same town in Schleswig Holstein but met in Woronesh. The wise guy in front of us is Fritz Kandler, and the redhead's name is Walter Arnold. Walter made the mistake of coming to Germany from America only a year before the war. He came for some inheritance. Nice mess he inherited." Hans kicked a small rock to the side. "If only he had become an American citizen before coming back here, he could have spent the war years in some comfortable internment camp inside Germany. But then he might have gotten it on his head from his own people." He made a gesture of bombs falling from the sky.

"Sounds crazy, doesn't it?" Hans added.

"It sure isn't funny," Walter said, slightly angered.

They had walked for almost an hour when Hans, glancing at Christine, suggested they rest for a while. They sat down on the grass. The soldiers passed their water-filled canteens around. Christine, too, took a drink.

"Do you have something to eat?" Gustav turned to Christine.

"I've got some bread," Christine answered. She opened the canvas bag that Harald had given her, extracted half a loaf of bread and gave it to Gustav. From inside his shirt he pulled out a field knife of the Hitler Youth.

"Brand new . . . swastika and all! Where did you find that? It's never been used!" Fritz held out his hand to get a closer look.

"Found it in a field. People throw these things out. It's not good to have them on you, too dangerous!" He reached out and Fritz handed the knife back to him. Gustav began to cut the bread and handed the slices around.

"How come you are traveling alone?" Gustav asked Christine, his mouth full of bread.

In a few sentences Christine told her story.

"Was that you brother at the station?"

Christine nodded.

"He's my oldest brother. He just came back from the eastern front. He told me to stay close to women and children while I travel, because traveling is too dangerous for a girl alone."

"You think women and children can protect you from the dangers of traveling alone?" Gustav asked in a slightly sarcastic tone, cutting himself another slice from Christine's bread.

"Not really, "Christine said, shaking her head. She looked at Gustav, but he avoided her eyes. She was suddenly afraid.

"But God can," she added quickly.

"Oh, can He?" Gustav laughed coarsely. "I'd like to give him a chance to prove it. "Well, what do you say, guys?"

He stretched himself and looked around. The other soldiers looked down and chewed slowly. No one spoke.

"Come on, let's go, or we'll miss our train!" Hans said, jumping up.

He grabbed the parcel with Christine's books and started to walk. The other soldiers rose slowly, Christine, too, got up. Gustav sat and stared at his folded hands. He got to his feet, brushing the dry grass from his trousers with his hands. He walked over to Christine, took her chin in his large hand and said:

"I was only kidding. You know that, don't you?" His eyes were wild and he breathed heavily. Still holding her face, tightening his grip, he shouted:

"Say something! You know I was only joking. I want you to say something!"

Christine nodded through tears.

"You are hurting me," she whispered. "Yes, I know you were only teasing me."

He dropped his hand.

"I'm sorry, if I scared you," he said. He picked up Christine's suitcase. "I'll carry that," he mumbled and began to walk.

Soon they could see the freight train to their far left. They crawled through the barbed wire fence of a cow pasture to get there faster. Karl-Heinz stumbled.

"Look what I found!" he called out. "*Mein Kampf,* Hitler's Bible, with the crest of the City of Magdeburg—Special Edition—printed in 1941. Look at this: Copyright 1925-27. I didn't know Hitler wrote that so early. If our parents had only read it! They had plenty of time to find out what he was up to. It says here: 6,900,000 copies printed so far. Incredible! And here is a special dedication: "To the newly married couple Hartmann-Geiser with best wishes for a happy life together, presented by the City of Magdeburg on 10 September 1941, signed, Mayor P. Hauser." I wonder where they are now. I'll take that with me." He started pushing the book in his bag. "The Americans like that kind of stuff."

"Don't be a fool!" Hans said, taking the book away from Karl-Heinz and throwing it back into the pasture. "If the Russians find that on you, you're dead."

Most wagons were overcrowded. Gustav, Karl-Heinz and Fritz climbed onto the train roof. Hans and Christine sat on the platform at the end of the railroad car usually reserved for train personnel. Christine dozed off, resting her head on her suitcase. When she awoke, they had already passed the city of Stendal. She looked at the passing countryside, meadows; little streams dividing potato fields and unplowed stubble fields, cow pastures and woods that offered an occasional glimpse of the red roofs of a small farm village.

"I like this land," Christine said. "It's so different from the *Magdeburger Boerde,* so much more alive. No big cities, no factories, it's so peaceful. Areas like this never change, no matter what goes on in the rest of the world. They are in tune with nature."

"City life has its advantages, too," Hans replied, looking into the distance. "It all depends."

They fell silent again, following their own thoughts.

"Germany is finished," Hans said suddenly, looking straight at Christine. "We don't have a future. This war—this is the end of Germany!" He shook his head. "You know, Hitler had many good ideas, especially in the beginning, like making Germany strong and prosperous again, but that thing with the camps, that was a big mistake. You've heard about the concentration camps, right?"

"Not much," Christine answered. "In the village where I grew up there was that man named Vogel and people always said: "If you don't keep your mouth shut, Mr. Vogel will get you into a concentration camp"—KZ they called it, but I've never known anyone who had to go there."

"Did you see the people boarding the train? The ones like skin and bones? They were probably in the camps. They might even be Jews."

" . . . Jews"?

"Yes. All the Jews were put in those camps. There were lots of camps in the east. I heard the Jews were killed there by the thousands, men, women, and children."

" . . . but why? What did they do?"

"Nothing, just because they were Jews, that's all. Hitler said they were enemies of the Reich . . . sub-humans."

Christine shuddered.

"I don't believe that." She paused, and then said:

"I've never met a Jew, what are they like?"

"Depends on where they live, in what country, and whether they are integrated or live in ghettos. I've met a lot of Jews in Duesseldorf. They weren't different from other people. Our doctor was a Jew. I didn't even know they were Jewish until one day when we were told they had left, resettled in the east. How come you have never met a Jew, Christine?"

"I grew up in that little village I told you about. There were only 99 people living in the whole town. We all went to the same Protestant Church on Sundays. When I entered high school in Wiedenbeck in 1940, there simply weren't any Jews, maybe they had left earlier?"

Hans nodded, looking straight ahead.

"Germany will have to pay for this for a long time," he said, looking down, "for a long, long time—maybe forever."

The towers of Wiedenbeck appeared on the horizon. The train slowed down and came to a halt under the open sky. Many people jumped from the train and disappeared in the nearby woods. Black and white cows and *Heidschnucken* sheep grazed peacefully.

The train started again, moving slowly into the station. Russian soldiers and German border police swarmed about to check the arriving passengers. Wiedenbeck was now a border town. German soldiers and refugees with valid papers to go west were sent to the right, local passengers and those traveling to Wiedenbeck and surrounding areas to the left side. Everything went smoothly. Those with false papers or no documents at all had left the train five minutes before.

Christine saw Grandfather's horse-drawn carriage through the gates of the exit on the other side of the street.

"Come see me in Duesseldorf!" Hans shouted as he moved to the right.

"I just might surprise you some day," Christine said, laughing, waving goodbye. She rushed to the exit and showed her papers to the young Russian soldier. He smiled at her without looking at the paper and waved her through.

She threw her suitcase and the package into the wagon and climbed up to the seat next to Grandfather. He hugged her awkwardly and adjusted the sheepskin around her back. He reached behind, picked up a horse-blanket and wrapped Christine into it to protect her from the biting wind.

"How did you know I was coming at this time, Grandfather?"

"A Mr. Alpert sent a message to the *Buergermeister*, it said: The chicken arrives today."

They both laughed.

Christine leaned back contentedly. Grandfather clicked his tongue. The horse jumped briefly, neighing as they drove away from the station.

They drove along the narrow cobblestone street towards *Bismarckstrasse*, then right on *Goethestrasse*, leaving the city to their left. *Goethestrasse* led directly to the highway, once a major road to Hamburg, but now, since the checkpoint was only eight kilometers away, traveled mainly by local farmers, refugees with valid papers going west, and Russian military vehicles.

Christine liked being with Grandfather. With him she felt protected and loved. He never talked much. His tall, lean frame exuded a quiet strength. His eyes, the color of a winter sky just before the snow, seemed to look through a person or into his heart, whichever he chose.

"Look at them! They look so tired," Grandfather interrupted her thoughts, pointing at two women and a little boy, walking on the road shoulder before them, bending under the load of their large rucksacks.

"Let's give them a lift!"

He veered over to the side and stopped.

"Going west?" he called. "Hop in!" he added before they could answer. He moved the blankets in the back to the left side. The women lifted their rucksacks on the wagon. They helped the little boy up and climbed in after him.

"That's a big rucksack you have," Grandfather said to the boy. "What's your name?"

"Michael . . . Michael Winter."

"You must be ten years old," Grandfather said with a smile.

"Eight," the boy answered. "I'm big." He stretched himself.

"You sure are, Michael, I bet you're a great help for your mother."

Michael nodded and smiled.

"Ladies, use the blankets, if you want, the wind is quite cold—east wind," he said, turning to the women. They huddled together under the blankets and the carriage started moving.

A few moments later they were approached by a Russian patrol.

"Pretend you are sleeping, ladies!" Grandfather spoke quickly—Russian border patrol!"

Instantly the women tilted their heads and closed their eyes. Michael looked frightened. Christine pulled the blanket up to her chin.

The Russian soldiers motioned with their hands for the carriage to stop. Grandfather moved onto the shoulder. One soldier walked up.

"*Kooda?*" he snapped.

"Domoy," Grandfather responded, using his newly acquired Russian.

"Documyente, pazhalsta!"

Grandfather fumbled for his papers and handed them to the soldier. While the first soldier was reading, the other looked into the wagon.

"Szemya?" he pointed to the women in the back and at Christine.

Grandfather gave him a puzzled look.

"Nye panimayoo," he said.

The soldier tried again, this time in German: *"Familie?"*

Grandfather nodded quickly.

"Yes—family, my daughters, my grandson Michael. Michael, shake hands with the gentlemen!" Michael, close to tears, shook the soldiers' hands. They laughed and one tickled him under the chin.

"This is my granddaughter," Grandfather pointed to Christine. "She's sick, very sick!"

The soldiers jumped back.

"Sick? Very sick! No good—very bad."

The first soldier, trying to avoid getting close to Christine, handed the papers back to Grandfather.

"Kharasho, Grandpa . . ." he said, and gestured for Grandfather to move on.

They continued on the poplar-lined asphalt road, passing several people on their way to the border, farmers on bicycles and wooden field wagons drawn by black and white colored cows. Green potato fields alternated with harvested rye fields. Soon they passed the first pine woods of Rebenau. Grandfather entered a narrow forest road that lead to the back of his property. Before the women and Michael left, he instructed them as to the best way to cross the border. Christine, too, listened very carefully.

Chapter 11

hristine inhaled the scent of the pine trees as the cart hobbled along the unpaved lane toward the back gate of the Lahrssen farm, Mother's childhood home. Nothing seemed to have changed. Chickens were picking at the compost heap near the barn back wall outside the gate. In front of the barn, inside the courtyard, was a dung hill where more chickens were feeding on the day's kitchen scraps. The pungent smell was overpowering. To the right was a row of sheds for geese, chickens and ducks. A water pump with a large water-filled trough stood outside the kitchen door. The dilapidated wooden outhouse, with a heart-shaped opening in the door, stood in the corner by the stables. Next to it, where the barn began, was the dog house. Nero, a large terrier with German shepherd ancestry, was tearing at his chain, barking incessantly, probably jealous of the ducks and geese frolicking in the water trough. Cows regurgitated behind barriers in the open stable door on the left. The neighing of two other horses was a sign that they had heard the carriage coming. The back of the house, with a second entrance to the wash house and baking chamber, and the large doorways on either side of the house leading into the street, completed the square.

Christine drew a deep breath. The smell of the stables, the dung heap and the moisture of the earth, mixed with that of onions fried in bacon, gave her a familiar comfortable feeling.

"It's wonderful, Grandfather!" she exclaimed. "Just as I remember it. And the war is over. No more blacking out the windows. Remember how the air raid warden always shouted at you because he could still see light in your windows? And how you shouted back that you have nothing against the British, so why should they bomb your house? The long-awaited peace has finally come."

She smiled at Grandfather, but his face remained serious.

"Yes," Grandfather began slowly. "Yes, the guns have stopped, but peace?" He shook his head. "This village has never been less at peace than it is now." He started to climb down the wagon. Turning around he said, his eyes filled with a deep sadness:

"And this is only the beginning."

Oma Anna came rushing down the kitchen steps.

"I'm so glad you are here!" She reached out to embrace Christine. "Let me look at you! Almost a young lady, but"—she looked into Christine's eyes and shook her head—"much too serious."

She picked up the suitcase from the carriage.

"Not much in here." Her voice was cheerful again. "It's rather light."

She turned toward the house, her wooden clogs clicking on the courtyard cobblestones. Grandfather unharnessed the horse and led it to the stable.

The living room was almost bare. Christine stared at the few coarsely constructed chairs and the unfinished wooden table. A multicolored crochet afghan, made from yarn scraps, was draped over the back of a chair.

"Where is all the furniture, Oma Anna?" Christine cried out. "And the rugs are gone, too!"

The furniture is under the straw in the barn," Oma Anna said in a low voice. "The rugs are in the upper barn under the hay. The occupation forces use the most comfortable homes for their officers. Some families, like our *Buergermeister,* the mayor, have been thrown out indefinitely." She lowered her voice even more. "Our silver and china have been buried in the garden since last April." She took a deep breath.

"I tell you, we couldn't have done it without the help of Jacques and Jean-Pierre."

Christine lowered her eyes.

Jaques and Jean-Pierre, where are they now?" Christine asked.

"They left the day the British arrived, happy to be free. I'll tell you all about that later," Oma Anna said, walking towards the small room next to the living room.

"You'll sleep here again, Christine." She paused. "Let me see, the last time you slept here was a couple of years ago. Am I right?"

Christine nodded.

The room was cold. Christine eyed the thick feather bedding longingly. Oma Anna placed the suitcase on top of the chest of drawers.

"Back to the kitchen, you need a hot drink, Christine," she ordered. "I also want to warm a brick for your bed in the tile oven."

She poured warm water into the porcelain bowl in the large square kitchen sink. Christine washed her face and hands. Grandfather was finishing the evening feeding begun earlier by Oma Anna. After a while he walked in, rolled up his sleeves and washed up. Oma Anna carried the black iron pot with steaming boiled potatoes to the table. She brought a large bowl of fresh milk from the storage room next to the kitchen. After Grandfather and Christine were seated, she took the iron skillet with the hot dip of onions fried in bacon and placed it on the table. They all bowed their heads in a brief silent prayer. They peeled the potatoes and dipped the pieces into the skillet. With their soup spoons they ate the milk directly from the big bowl.

"So many men have already come home," Oma Anna said. "I'm surprised you still haven't heard from your father. Wasn't he stationed in Magdeburg? That's not far from Bahrenberg."

"Last year he was, for a while," Christine replied.

"Yes, I remember. He had one of you children come to Magdeburg once a week to take home the *Kommissbrot* he had salvaged from the field bakery to help your mother get over the time when she had used up all your bread rations." She paused.

"How was it when they came to Bahrenberg? The Russians, I mean?" She spoke again.

"Better than we had expected," Christine said. "Not like east of the Elbe where they lived by the slogan: The German women are your reward! But, of course, we weren't sure in the beginning. We were quite frightened."

She fell silent.

"They say that our troops had not behaved any better in Russia," Oma Anna said. "I can't believe that. But who are we to open our mouth? We have lost the war. The victor is always right."

"There's so much about the war we don't know," Grandfather said. "With only one station to listen to, how could we have found out? And the BBC, the British Broadcast Company, I always had a lot of disturbance with that."

He peeled another potato.

"You see, according to our own news, we were winning all the time. How then could we have lost the war? We were still "winning," when the Russians stood at our gates! Maybe we'll hear about that someday." He looked angry and Oma and Christine felt it was better to change the subject.

"What happened to Jacques and Jean-Pierre?" Christine asked after a long silence.

"They left the day the British arrived. You should have seen how Jacques hugged me and swirled me around that day, singing: 'It's a long way to Tipperary . . . Oma Anna said, her eyes sparkling. "The British soldiers sang it all the time."

She shook her head, her eyes far away.

"What a day it was! What a day! And then he said: "Oma Anna, someday I'll be back with my family, and when you can travel again, I want you both to come to Brussels. I'll bake the finest cake for you!'""

She paused.

"But now, with the Russians here and trying to close the borders, I doubt that we'll ever get to go."

"But they can't close the border forever, maybe for a while until they have taken what they want. Then all the troops will go back to their countries, back to their families," Christine suggested.

"They'll probably stay for a few years," Grandfather said. "They don't go through all the trouble of establishing the border for just a few months. All that hassle about the Russians stopping at the Elbe. It took months until the

Americans and the Russians could finally agree on how far the Russians could go west. Someday the western powers will regret that they let the Russians come in so far." He shook his head. "The people of Bavaria, where all the mess started, are the lucky ones. The Americans are bringing in a lot of aid, CARE they call it, mostly food, I think."

There was a long silence.

Christine thought of the summer of 1943. One morning she had woken up and found a box of exquisite chocolates on her bedcover. And she had asked Oma Anna where they had come from.

"Jacques received his monthly package from home," Oma Anna had replied. "He owns a pastry shop in Brussels, the finest."

And Christine had suddenly shouted:

"I cannot take this! A German girl does not accept gifts from an enemy of the Great Reich! Don't you know we are not allowed to take anything from a prisoner-of war? If someone reports this, we'll be punished, maybe even shot!"

Oma Anna had called Jacques and he had removed the chocolates without a word, not looking at either of them. The next morning there were several bars of milk chocolate on the bed. Oma Anna was standing by her bed, a threatening statue come alive, unlike her usual gentle nature.

"Bu . . . bu . . . but . . ." Christine stammered. "I . . . I told you . . ."

And Oma Anna had cut her short in her sternest voice:

"You hurt Jacques yesterday! Whatever they teach you out there, it is WRONG! Can't you see these people are human beings, too? Jacques has a daughter your age."

Christine had looked up and seen Grandfather standing in the door frame, Jacques right behind him, his large, ruddy face drawn. And Oma Anna had bent down, whispering:

"Jacques is our friend."

When she had seen Christine's shocked expression, she added quickly:

"This is our secret. I trust you to keep it to yourself."

She had turned around and walked to the door. Walking away, Grandfather had mumbled:

"That Austrian monkey is killing the souls of our children."

Christine could not fall asleep for a long time. The secret her beloved grandparents had burdened her with was almost too hard to bear. She knew she had to choose between her grandparents with their anti-government behavior and her duty as a German girl to report such actions immediately. She chose her grandparents. She never mentioned the incident to anyone, but wondered if these political differences were not the reason for the animosity between Papa and Grandfather.

"Jean-Pierre never liked us, did he, Oma?" Christine spoke into the silence. "He always looked angry. He never talked. Well, he liked YOU," she added hastily. "He always called you 'Mother.'"

Oma Anna nodded.

'Yes," she mused. "Jean Pierre was a very troubled young man. He was only twenty when he became a prisoner-of-war. His younger brother had been picked up by the SS on his way to school in Marseille. He was found shot a few days later. Nobody knew why. He was only seventeen years old. That was all he ever said about his family. I never dared to ask about his parents. But then, he couldn't speak German and refused to learn it. Jacques was almost fluent in German when he left. For him it came easy. He spoke Flemish and that's much like our *Plattdeutsch*. She paused, nodding. "Yes, Jean-Pierre was very bitter."

Around eight o'clock, Grandfather and Oma Anna had just finished closing the stables, when the electricity was cut off. When it had not come back by 9:30, Oma Anna stirred the ashes in the stove to extinguish the fire and they all went to bed. The warm brick covered with newspaper wrapping was already under Christine's bedcovers. She said good night and felt her way through the dark living room to her tiny bedroom. She undressed quickly, putting on the white linen nightgown Mrs. Kohler had given her. Slipping into her comfortable warm bed, she fell asleep before she had time to think about the day's events.

The next morning Christine awoke early. Was it from the cock's crowing? Or from the clattering of the milk cans Grandfather carried to the milk bench in front of the house for collection by the village milk wagon for the dairy in Wiedenbeck? Or perhaps from the sound of boots on the cobblestone street, made by the Russian border guards to and from their shifts at the border, only two kilometers away?

Christine jumped up and dipped her hands into the cold water in the washbowl on the chest of drawers. She wet her face and dried it, braided her long hair and walked out to the kitchen to brush her teeth with warm water. Through the open door she could hear Grandfather talking to the horses. She put on her sweater and a pair of bulky pants. She looked in the mirror, but turned away quickly, almost hearing Mother say: "Only girls who think more of their body than of their mind look at themselves." She put on the army socks Papa had brought home on his last furlough and her only pair of shoes. She went through the kitchen to the stables, first to the cow stable. Oma Anna was sitting on a little round wooden stool milking a cow. She smiled at Christine, took the white enamel cup from a stool next to her and filled it directly from the udder.

"Come, drink it," she offered. "It'll make you strong!"

Christine shook her head.

"Mother says, milk has to be boiled, otherwise we'll get tuberculosis."

"It's all right. Look, I drink it! Our cows are healthy. It tastes even better this way." She pressed the cup into Christine's hand. "Last night's milk wasn't boiled."

Christine brought the cup to her lips and began to sip. The milk, still warm from the cow's body, had a slightly nutty flavor, but the body warmth bothered Christine. She put the cup on the milking stool and said:

"I'll see what Grandfather is doing."

Relieved she left the stable.

Quickly the village came alive. At the sound of a whistle, Grandfather opened the heavy courtyard door to the right. The geese and ducks had already lined up and raced out of the door to join the stream of other fowl on their way to the village pond. A boy of fourteen walked behind them with a long willow branch to keep them on the path, which was not really necessary since they just followed the ones in front of them. Another youth, Wolfgang, about the same age, arrived at seven at the Lahrssen's to take the cows out to graze.

Christine had met him two summers ago when he had helped her grandparents during the grain harvest.

"Can I go with Wolfgang, Grandfather?"

"Sure, go ahead, Christine," Grandfather called from the barn. "I'll pick you up around noon on my way back from the Schuster farm. The old ladies need help. Wolfgang will stay out there. The fence is broken in too many places."

Christine and Wolfgang followed the twelve cows, counting the calves. Other cowherds joined the procession, all at a leisurely pace. The powerful smell of a mixture of damp soil and manure lay over the village. The cows knew their way. Only occasionally a young one tried to disappear in a side street and had to be brought back. Each group of cows had a different and distinctive sound of bells for easy identification. Chickens and birds feasted on horse manure in the street, waiting until the last moment before dispersing.

"*Altmaerker* Symphony," Christine remarked. "They don't have that in the Magdeburger Boerde. There are no meadows with grass and wildflowers like here, or woods with violets, primroses, and forget-me-nots, or houses with a large wheel for a stork's nest on the roof, or the calling of a cuckoo in the spring." She looked around. From any road in the village one could see the distant woods, oaks and beech trees on one side, pine woods interspersed with gentle white birches on the other.

"The Altmark has a soul," she said, looking at Wolfgang.

" . . . a soul?"

She nodded. She felt it was no use explaining this to Wolfgang. He would not know what she meant.

They passed the *Schuhmacher's Gasthaus* on the right, and, next to it, the mayor's large house. Russian soldiers, some with short weapons, others with rifles, moved in and out of the building. Some stood and watched the activities in the street, talking to each other, chatting and laughing. A few sat on the milk bench in front of the mayor's house, their military caps tilted all the way to the back of their heads.

"Lots of Russians here," Wolfgang whispered. "Somebody said that, as soon as they train German border guards, they'll use half and half. Right now they have only a few Germans at the border, mostly former military."

"Tell me, Wolfgang, is the border close to where we are going?"

"Very close."

"Have you ever gone across?"

"Lots of times."

"Ever been caught?"

Wolfgang shook his head. "I can run fast," he said.

"What happens when they catch you?"

He shrugged his shoulders. "Take you to the *Kommandantura*, I guess."

"Do your parents know that you've been across?"

Wolfgang stopped and looked at Christine in disbelief.

"You think I'm crazy? I asked my father once if I can go with the others." 'Absolutely not,' he had shouted. 'This is not a game, it is dangerous.' You know, old people are always scared."

The cows stopped briefly by the pond. Geese and ducks screamed and raced to the other side as the cows walked into the water. A few minutes later the cows were back on the road and peace returned to the pond.

After walking for about fifteen minutes past pastures, each one surrounded by a rough wooden or barbed wire fence, Wolfgang ran ahead to open the wide wooden gate of the Lahrssen pasture. He closed it as soon as Christine and the cows had entered. They shooed the cows away and sat down on a felled tree. The cows began to graze.

"Grandfather says that it is difficult for the farmers here," Christine said. "Most farmers have barely enough for themselves. The soil is too sandy. No matter how hard they work, they barely have enough to live on."

And he had told Christine that this area used to be called the "sandbox of the Holy Roman Empire of the German Nation," because Elector Joachim Friedrich never could get any money from the farmers. Not much had changed since the 16th century, but Christine knew her grandparents were part of this land; they would never even think of being elsewhere.

"It's over there," Wolfgang interrupted her thoughts, "the border!" He pointed to a group of trees to their left. "It's somewhere behind those trees. I don't know exactly where. There are no signs."

"Can we go up there?" Christine got up.

"Sure."

"How far can we go?"

Wolfgang was now standing, too.

"There's a ditch in front of the trees. Perhaps we shouldn't cross that, but that far we can go." Wolfgang suggested.

"Why don't we see any guards?"

"Do you think they stand there for everyone to see? They are hiding, waiting for someone to cross, and then ... wham!"

Christine felt the excitement building up in her as they walked toward the ditch.

"Let's just put one foot in the water and see what happens," she said.

They looked around. They were alone. They jumped across the ditch, threw themselves onto the grassy embankment and started looking through the underbrush. And there, Christine could not believe her eyes, were two men in green uniforms, chatting.

"Are they from the east or west?" she whispered.

Wolfgang shrugged his shoulders and placed his index finger on his lips.

The uniformed men stopped talking and listened, looking around. The youngsters put their heads on the ground and slid down the embankment leaving only their heads above the edge. Christine did not dare breathe. She pressed her eyes close. Her heart was pounding. She was certain it would stop any moment.

She slowly opened her eyes. A pair of shiny black boots—right before her eyes! She could smell the polished leather.

Her eyes traveled upwards where the leather met with the green trousers stuffed into the boots, and higher and higher along the green uniform to a pinkish area, the face.

O God, border police! I don't want to be arrested. What if they beat me? Or shoot? Or drag me away?

She had forgotten about Wolfgang. All she was aware of was this threatening giant in a green uniform in front of her. She gasped for air.

I've lost my voice!

"Get up!" the guard barked after a long silence filled with tension.

Christine could not move.

I'm paralyzed! Oh God!

"I said, get up!" the motionless giant shouted. They both scrambled to their feet.

"Don't you know you are not supposed to be here? Really, your father should whip you!"

He was a tall man in his forties, wearing the German military uniform without insignias.

"People have been killed in this area, and not by border police, but by criminals." He lowered his voice. "If I ever catch you here again, you won't get off that easily. Now . . . get lost!"

He made a gesture of chasing them away. They started to run, slowing down after a while.

"Were they from the east or west, Wolfgang?" Christine asked again.

"I don't know," Wolfgang replied. "They all wear the same green uniform. I don't think you can tell until you ask them or they tell you, but I think they were from the west. I saw them smiling when they left."

"They've found another woman in the Rhode's potato field," Grandfather said during supper. "Strangled and raped; pots and pans all over the place. Her open suitcase was found about ten meters away, purse gone. No identification. It looks like another case of a woman alone, trusting one of those so-called border guides who promise to take them to the west."

He paused.

"It's the fourth in three months. The police are trying to find out who she is so they can notify her family. They've laid her out in the old windmill."

"How awful!" Christine gasped, turning pale.

Grandfather nodded.

Three days later the woman was quietly buried in the village cemetery. There were no flowers. Just a roughly hewn cross with a cardboard inscription:

"Unknown Woman—approx. 36 years old; blond, blue eyed. Found dead at the border on 15 September, 1945."

Chapter 12

On Monday, October 1ˢᵗ, Grandfather harnessed the horses at daybreak to take Christine to Wiedenbeck. On Sunday Christine had visited a former classmate, Hella Schulz, to find out if Hella would go back to school.

"No," Hella had said. "I've had enough of school. I'll stay home and help Mother. My father is still missing in Stalingrad, and since our foreign laborers left, my mother and I have to do everything ourselves. We haven't even plowed our stubble fields yet and soon the potato fields will have to be harvested. I don't plan to attend a university anyway," she paused briefly. "But I'm glad you're here, Christine. Let's go to the Saturday night dances some time!"

A veil of fog rose above the moist earth on both sides of the road. The crisp autumn wind rustled in the poplar trees lining the highway, the *Wiedenbecker Chaussee.*

Many vehicles were on the road despite the early hour, farm carts like theirs, but mainly Russian military three-quarter ton trucks, filled with Russian soldiers,

German and Russian border guards on bicycles and people on foot.

Christine, wrapped in a large black and white checkered horse blanket, which she held together under her chin, was thinking about Grandfather. There he was sitting next to her. His lower face was largely covered by a dark-brown beard and a huge mustache. His back was slightly bent and his labor-worn hands held the reins between his knees. A thick grey scarf, knit by Oma Anna was tucked into his heavy black coat that showed large grey patches on the elbows. Christine knew so little about him and the rest of the family. Only when the food situation had begun to worsen, had Papa finally allowed contact with Mother's family. Before that, the children knew almost nothing about their relatives. Christine remembered how, one day in autumn 1943, Mother had begged Papa to let her go home to visit her parents whom she had not seen for over fifteen years even though they lived only twenty kilometers away. Soon afterwards, Mother had taken the children for a visit, much to Papa's dislike. From then on the children were always welcome to spend their school vacation at their grandparents' farm.

"At least they can get enough to eat," Papa had said.

But he had cautioned Mother to make it clear to her parents that they must speak High German in front of the children, otherwise the children would not be allowed to go. Christine had asked Papa why he disliked their grandparents so much.

"It's not Oma Anna," he had said. "It's your Grandfather, I mean, your step-Grandfather," he said, emphasizing the 'step.' "He just never treated your mother well."

But from Mother, Christine had heard just the opposite, that he was the kindest man she had ever known.

"I think it's because Grandfather does not like the Hitler government," Mother had whispered. "Papa thinks Grandfather will get us all in trouble and Papa, being an employee of the government, might even lose his job—or more. We are being watched all the time."

When Christine finally met Grandfather, she knew Mother had spoken the truth. He had wept openly when he embraced Mother the day she brought the children the first time. For hours he had played Rummy and Checkers with them.

Since Christine was one of the older children who could already help in the fields, she was allowed to spend the six weeks summer vacation in 1943 in Rebenau. Harald preferred to stay close to his friend whose father had a veterinary clinic. He wanted to be a veterinarian someday.

"I like the *Plattdeutsch* you speak," Christine had told Oma Anna the first time Oma struggled with the High German she rarely spoke. "Speak it for me! I like to learn different dialects and languages . . . and don't worry, I won't tell Papa."

Oma Anna had smiled and gone back to her dialect without hesitation.

Then there was Uncle Hans, Mother's brother. Christine had met him only once during his furlough from the Russian front. He was missing since the battle of Woronesh. It was his room Christine was now occupying. A younger daughter, Mother's half-sister, had married a German army officer and moved to Thuringia. Now Grandfather and Oma Anna lived alone.

"So, what do you want to do after you graduate?" Grandfather interrupted her thoughts.

"I want to learn many foreign languages," Christine replied, excitement in her voice." I would like to become an interpreter some day and travel all over the world. I'd like to see the Louvre in Paris, and Big Ben in London, and Julia's Balcony in Verona, and the Pieta in St. Peter's in Rome, and the Villa San Michele on Capri, and—and—and!" She paused, turning serious. "But then, so much has changed. It looks like we won't be able to move for a long time. I really don't know now."

She shrugged her shoulders. Turning to Grandfather, she asked:

"What would you do, Grandfather, if you were my age?"

Grandfather gazed into the distance.

"You see," he began slowly, "a farmer is like a tree. His roots are in his soil. No matter how strong he is, or how strong the forces are that draw him away, he can only bend. He cannot leave. He would die."

He paused, then said:

"But you, Christine, you are young and free. You have a beautiful dream. Don't let go of it! No matter how impossible it may seem now."

Grandfather did not know then, nor did he suspect, that less than five years later all he owned would be swallowed up by the Communist Land Reform Program. He would be a farmer without a land, a paid farm laborer on his own land, the land that had been in his family for over 400 years.

Yes, Christine had a dream. In a few months she would be seventeen. No one knew what the future might hold, but one thing she knew, she would not sit back and let things happen. Germany was largely destroyed, and so many people had perished because a madman had come to power, with all the decent and law-abiding citizens only concerned with their immediate affairs. What if the Russians closed the borders so tightly that no one could get out? No, that could not happen! Not with the Americans being friends with the Russians and watching it all. Their belief in freedom was too strong.

Should she go to Western Germany? Could she really leave her family behind, perhaps never to see them again? She shook her head. Occupation is never permanent, Grandfather had said. The troops might stay for months, or even years, until they have taken what they want, but then they would all go home. Those young soldiers don't want to be in a foreign country either.

She looked at the green fields, divided by narrow streams lined with young willows. The leaves, turning brown, tried to hold on to the slim sturdy branches pointing to the sky. A few dry ones danced along the street like children on a playground, until a gust lifted them up, carrying them across the field. No, she wouldn't leave, she couldn't. Her life was here. Where would she go, anyway? True, she had classmates in the west, but she would never ask anyone to live with them. Nobody had enough to feed an extra mouth. And she would not get ration cards if she went over illegally, under age, without her parents or their permission. But it was nice to dream about the world out there, a world she had read about so often, the world that had touched her briefly when the Americans came to Bahrenberg in April 1945.

Wiedenbeck, 2km, the sign said. Christine could see the sun rising behind the spires of St. Mary's Church, but it would be a while before it would warm the air.

"All these women and children with rucksacks, are they going to the border, Grandfather?"

"No, Christine, they are *Hamsterfrauen.* They are city women. Every day they go to the villages in hope of getting food from the farmers in exchange for pieces of clothing, jewelry, silver, stockings or other items the farmers could use. I'm glad we live farther away. These city people don't realize that we have a quota to fill."

They passed the settlement houses on both sides of the road, with their little flower gardens in the front and a vegetable patch on the side or in the back. The flower boxes outside the windows were bursting with asters and mums, their golden color enhanced by the touch of the sunrays under an almost cloudless sky. A few anti-tank obstacles, hastily erected by the *Volkssturm* during the final days of the war, lay dismantled by the side of the road.

Soon they entered the city limits. Gracious old three-story homes with large beech and oak trees in front on a well-kept lawn with an occasional round flower bed, told of a prosperous past. Only the bullet-riddled side walls reminded the passer-by of recent war action. Through the gap between the houses Christine could see a few railroad cars on the tracks with bold lettering: RAEDER MUESSEN ROLLEN FUER DEN SIEG (Wheels must roll for Victory!). Underneath, someone had scribbled in letters of almost equal size: UND KINDERWAGEN FUER DEN NAECHSTEN KRIEG (And baby carriages for the next war!)

They drove through the Karl's Gate, a thick-walled brick archway, built almost seven hundred years before. The cold, damp air from the musty niches that never saw the sun made Christine shiver. After they passed the large Father Jahn Sports Hall, located in walking distance from all the schools, Grandfather turned right and drove directly to the tall, square brick building with spires on each of the four corners of the roof. A large clock with Roman numerals loomed directly above the concrete sign: JOHANNES BRAHMS OBERSCHULE FUER MAEDCHEN (Johannes

Brahms High School for Girls}. The heavy wooden gate with large metal hinges was closed.

Christine stepped from the carriage to read the paper attached to the door. It said that the school had not been disinfected after being used as a military hospital and, later on, as refugee shelter. Registrants should go to the boys' high school, the ALBRECHTS GYMNASIUM.

Only one third of Christine's former classmates showed up to register. All those now living in the British Zone would not return. They would go to a new school in the west. Since it was not mandatory to attend school after the age of fourteen, many simply stayed home. There were numerous newcomers, refugees, displaced persons; ethnic Germans expelled from Russia, Poland, and Romania whose spoke little German. There were also children of anti-Nazis, whose fathers or other family members had been arrested after the attempt on Hitler's life on July 20, 1944. At that time those children had been expelled from all institutions of higher learning all over Germany.

The students learned that Dr. Auerbach, their principal, as well as their English teacher Miss Hempler, had left with the British occupation troops. Most of the other teachers would, for the time being, return. They also learned that, from now on, the schools would not charge any fees and that the schools would be co-ed. No one would graduate the following spring but be kept in school another year. The Russian language would be taught except in the two upper grades. The older students would concentrate on their academics and catch up with the curriculum, since there had been too many interruptions and cancellations due to air alerts.

Rosemarie von Hartenstein, a classmate since 1940, grabbed Christine by the arm.

"Come here, Christine! I must show you something! You won't believe this. Look at that list! Yes, you are reading right, Olsheimer is coming back."

This history teacher had been the most hated teacher at the school. A tall *Walkuere*-type woman, her colorless face with large wire-rimmed glasses over button eyes topped by a thick grey braid wrapped around her head, she had taught them how to jump up "like one man" when she entered the classroom and raise the right arm high and shout in unison: "*Heil Hitler, Fraeulein Olsheimer*!" Those who had shouted a little too early or too late would have to step to the wall, their backs turned to the class. Then she would walk around with a ruler and measure the angle of the arm. Inevitably, she would stop by Rosemarie and adjust her arm with the ruler, hissing: "I'll teach you yet!"

"I'm going to get her!" Rosemarie whispered to Christine, her eyes flashing. "Yes, I'm going to get her, if it's the last thing I'll ever do!"

Before Christine could respond, Rosemarie was gone.

Three hours later Christine sat in the *Stadt Café* across from the *Rathaus*, waiting for Grandfather. In the run-down establishment the aroma of steaming hot *ersatz kaffee* created a homey atmosphere. The waitress brought Christine the *Limonade* she had ordered, a raspberry-colored soft drink without fizz, called *Bonbonwasser* by the students because of its sickening sweet taste. Christine went through the papers distributed at school.

"Anything else?" the waitress asked.

Christine thought for a moment.

"No, thank you, *Fraeulein*," she said. She had decided to rather not waste a 10-gram bread ration stamp for a little piece of cake. Most customers were housewives with shopping nets and bags, resting up from their daily hunt for food, exchanging information on which store might have food tomorrow. They had the ration cards, but that did not mean that they could buy anything, the stores were usually empty.

The wide-hipped middle-aged waitress smiled as Grandfather walked in. He strode directly to Christine's table.

"*Guten Tag, Herr Lahrssen,*" the waitress called out, "the usual?" Grandfather was well known here. Every time he came to town he stopped here before returning home. The waitress brought his cup of *ersatz*-coffee.

"Marie, this is my granddaughter Christine," Grandfather said.

The waitress studied Christine's face.

"Yeah, I see the resemblance." She kept looking at Christine. "The same eyes, same thick brown hair."

Grandfather smiled amused since he had nothing to do with Christine's looks.

"I didn't see too many of the Russian soldiers out today," he whispered.

"They're in their barracks. Can't turn them loose on payday, I guess. She placed her hand on her hip and, holding onto the back of Grandfather's chair with the other hand, bent down and said in a low voice:

"Even though you don't see them, you feel them everywhere. But as long as they leave us alone, what more can we want?" She gestured as if shooing a fly away. "Savages they are, just savages!" Resuming an erect posture, she said, aloud:

"Will there be anything else, *Herr* Lahrssen?"

"That's it for today," Grandfather said, fumbling in his pocket as she walked away with the dishes. He brought out a little package and put it on the table, next to the money.

He waved goodbye to the owner and the waitress as he and Christine walked out the door.

"Every time I come here I leave a little liverwurst for her. Her husband is dead, killed in a railroad accident; and that during a time where everyone else is shot or bombed dead. And her little boy loves liverwurst."

Christine nodded. She, too, liked it, on Oma Anna's freshly baked bread, with slices of tomatoes on top.

Christine went to bed early that evening. Her body was tired, but her mind stimulated by the events of the day. She just needed to be alone.

What did she mean? I have never seen Rosemarie von Hartenstein so fiercely determined. She looked like a revolutionary with her large flashing gray eyes. What did she mean by 'I'm going to get her?'

Christine leaned back. It was great to be young and alive.

Chapter 13

The reopening of the schools was an important step toward the new Germany. Youth was to be education for a future in a free country. There was hope. There was a view of the future instead of the memory of a disastrous past. Students talked with animation in the corridors before classes began.

"I'll never understand how Germany could be so totally defeated. We were so victorious in the beginning."

"Hitler should have stayed out of Russia."

"Starting war with America was committing suicide!"

"It wasn't the *Fuhrer's* fault we lost. The military stabbed him in the back."

There was no end to the high school students trying to analyze what went wrong.

Every morning at 6 o'clock, Christine mounted Grandfather's rusty bicycle and left for school. Oma Anna helped her lift the bike down the front steps. She lit the carbide lamp in the center of the handle bar and watched until the soft light had disappeared in the distance. The black-top highway was strewn with wet brown leaves. The early morning fog hovered above the fields and the cow pastures. The air was heavy with the musty smell of decaying leaves and damp soil. Christine tried to ignore the jeering of the young Russian soldiers passing her on military vehicles. With each new day she could feel more and more the falling temperatures as the damp cold made her hands tingle as if stung by a thousand needles, turning them a bright red.

Confusion marked the first weeks of school, despite careful planning by the education authorities. During the first school days most of the old teachers were present, except those who had fled to the west. New teachers were brought in gradually, others left without explanation. The constant shifting made teaching and learning impossible. New students arrived almost daily, mainly from the east. Others disappeared, probably to the west. Even though boys and girls were now in the same school building, co-education was postponed for a while. It was not even considered for the two upper grades. The only time girls and boys saw each other was during recess. The girls walked arm in arm up and down the courtyard. The boys stood in the farthest corner by the fence, pretending the girls weren't even there. A few looked over but turned back quickly to concentrate on the conversation with their classmates. Teachers alternated supervising the students during recess. Visibly bored, they stalked up and down the courtyard, not speaking to anyone unless required to keep order.

Miss Olsheimer, the history teacher, and Miss Benkendorf, who taught German and geography, seemed to have the hardest time to adjust. They were the first to obtain new teaching materials, beginning with old books from which Nazi propaganda had been removed.

"You've probably forgotten everything I ever taught you," chirped Mrs. Heinrich, now a war widow, teacher of mathematics, physics and chemistry. "But since my subjects are non-political, I'll straighten you out in no time at all."

Adjusting her wire-rimmed glasses on her upturned nose she looked squarely at Christine.

"Am I seeing right? Yes, indeed, it is Christine Bachmann, my problem-child for years."

Blushing, Christine looked down, feeling the stares of the whole class on her. Her head felt hot, ready to burst.

"Perhaps those teachers in Magdeburg were more successful in teaching you the art of logical thinking," her voice stabbed at Christine.

The students looked away when they saw how embarrassed she was. Christine took a deep breath. How convenient an air alert would be now to interrupt this awful moment. But those times were over. Why did this monster ever come back? She should have gone out with the old regime. And Olsheimer too! I wonder if Rosemarie will ever do what she planned, or is still planning. I wish I had her guts. Besides, *who needs Cosinus and Sinus and old Pythagoras once you are grown up? But I do need math for graduation . . . at least a C.*

Mrs. Heinrich had turned to the class, talking incessantly. Christine did not hear one word, just constant rattling.

"Well, ladies—because that's what you are supposed to be now—" Christine heard her again.

The bell sounded for recess, interrupting whatever Mrs. Heinrich was going to tell "the ladies." They rushed out of the door before the bell had stopped. Christine got up slowly, waiting until the teacher had left the room. She felt a light tap on her shoulder.

"I'll help you with math," a voice whispered. "It's my favorite subject."

Christine turned around, wondering what a girl looked like whose favorite subject was math.

"I'm Sonia Hazek," he girl said, reaching out to shake Christine's hand. "I'm new here. I'm from Upper Silesia."

She was a mixture of a young girl and an old woman, Christine decided. Thick dark eyebrows spanned across watery blue eyes that accentuated her pale tired skin. A cluster of dark curls was held in place by a large kerchief.

"From Upper Silesia?" Christine shook the girl's hand. "I knew a boy from that area once—very briefly, I mean, I didn't really know him, but I've always wondered what became of him. I met him on the train. He just walked up to me and pushed a picture into my hand and whispered: "Pray for us—they're after us." And then he was gone. I turned the photo around and read: Erich Birnbaum and Mother. And there was an address. I can't remember the town, but I could read Upper Silesia. It was really strange."

"When was that?" Sonia asked.

"In 1940, my mother and I were on our way to register me for high school in Wiedenbeck."

"Probably Jews," Sonia said matter-of-factly. "There was a lot of that going on in my home town."

She adjusted her kerchief to stop the curls from falling over her face.

'We can sit on a bench in the Albrecht's Park every afternoon after school, if you want." Sonia paused when she noticed that Christine was not listening. "Our mathematics lesson, I mean, we can start next week—or tomorrow, if you like."

Christine nodded.

"Thank you, Sonia, that's very nice of you. I hope you realize that you are dealing with a hopeless case."

Sonia laughed, showing a mouthful of decaying teeth.

"Don't worry!" she said. "Whatever I set out to do, I never stop until it is completed. We'll start tomorrow!"

In the evening Christine looked at the photo of Erich Birnbaum and his mother. Somehow she had just never been able to throw it out. It had become her constant companion as she kept wondering what had become of them.

During the math sessions Christine learned that Sonia had, two years before, contracted typhus and had lost all her hair. She had alternately worn a wig or just a kerchief tied like a turban, until her hair had grown back after a few months, thicker and shinier than before, and now she had trouble controlling her curls. She had been evacuated from a hospital when the Russian troops approached her home town. During their *trek* to the west, she and her family had passed through a war zone and she had become separated from her two brothers and three sisters. Her mother had died of typhus before the evacuation, and her father was at the front somewhere. She had placed an application with a search service to find her remaining family, and she was confident that one day they would be reunited. Meanwhile she was living in Wiedenbeck with a couple that took in refugee children.

"I can see on your face that you are not listening, Christine," Sonia said. "Math is a logical science. There's no room for dreaming."

One afternoon, as Christine was unlocking her bicycle from the fence post, someone called her name. Turning around, she saw Heinz Gose, one of the boys from Rastenbeck, an elementary school class mate.

"Christine! What a surprise!" Heinz came running towards her. "I had no idea you were coming back to Wiedenbeck."

"Neither did I," Christine replied. "My school in Magdeburg was bombed out during the summer vacation last year."

They looked at each other for a moment.

"Somehow you've changed," Heinz said slowly. "Yet, then again, you are very much like I remember you. No more hide and seek in the dark, I take it?" They both laughed.

"How come you still have your braids? Don't you want to grow up?" Heinz teased.

"I have to keep them until my father comes home," Christine said. "He is still a prisoner-of war somewhere, we think. My mother says Papa might be too shocked when he suddenly sees me with an *Einheitsfrisur,* the standard hairdo, you know, five centimeters from your hair roots all around, the same for everybody." Christine drew a circle around her head with her index finger.

"Your father a soldier?" Heinz asked, sounding surprised. "I can't believe it. No wonder we lost the war!" He shook his head. "He sure knew how to give orders. I find it hard to believe that he ever learned to take any." He paused.

"If he doesn't come back, you'll have to run around with your braids all your life, I guess."

Christine was eager to change the subject.

"Tell me, did Mr. Vogel . . . did he make it through the war?"

"He made it through the war all right—to the day, in fact."

"What do you mean?"

Heinz placed his book bag on the ground and sat down. He motioned for Christine to sit next to him.

"He was killed the day before the British came. That evening the foreign laborers went to the Vogels' house. You should have seen it, a ghostly procession. In the light of the lanterns we could see the pitchforks and axes they were carrying over their shoulders."

"Oh, my God, what happened then?" Christine moaned.

"Well, the house was dark when they go there. They called for Mr. Vogel and his family to come out, but nothing happened. They banged their fists on the front door, shouting angry words. Most villagers stood outside, watching from afar. The laborers called again, telling Mrs. Vogel to come out with the boy, they would not be harmed."

He paused, taking a deep breath.

"And then the door opened slowly and the two came out. The people stepped aside to let them go through. Moments after the angry mob pressed into the open door, screaming and shouting. And then Mr. Vogel appeared on the balcony in his nightgown, and he tried to climb onto the roof. And he screamed . . . and in the dark it was just horrible. Some laborers were pulling on his nightshirt, and on the balcony they struggled with him, oh, and those screams! Then we heard a loud thump. Someone had pushed him, or he had fallen through the broken wooden balcony boards. When he hit the ground, the waiting crowd rushed forward. The shouting and screaming and gurgling! Just horrible! Horrible!"

Heinz shook his head.

"How awful!" Christine mumbled.

"Well, he asked for it, didn't he?" Heinz said. "You remember how he beat the Poles?"

"That's true, but…" Christine hesitated. "Yes, he deserved punishment . . . but this?"

Heinz jumped up.

"I'd better run, I don't want to miss my train," he said, shaking Christine's hand to say goodbye. "I'll see you again soon. And—don't waste another thought on him, he was the devil himself."

Chapter 14

Almost four weeks had passed since Christine's arrival in Rebenau. Grandfather had harvested apples, pears and plums, and Oma Anna had canned them, and arranged the apples on wooden racks in the cellar for winter storage. The sweet aroma of fruit drying in the air welcomed Christine every afternoon when she returned from school. Oma Anna had cleaned the large copper kettle and cooked *Pflaumenmus,* the delicious plum jam that was always on the breakfast table. She would stand for hours in the wash house, stirring the sweet mass until she could finally ladle it into the earthen crocks lined up on a wooden bench by the wall.

Grandfather had shorn the eight sheep, packed the wool in sack cloth bags, and stacked it in a corner of the barn. After the Russian occupation forces had chosen their permanent lodging, Grandfather had brought the furniture from the barn back into the house. The silver and good china, however, remained buried in the back yard.

Christine returned from school at 2:30 in the afternoon, except on Saturdays, when the schools let out at 12:00. After finishing her homework she helped with cleaning the house, since Oma Anna spent much time in the field harvesting potatoes and helping Grandfather with mending fences. On Saturdays, Oma Anna would get up at 4 o'clock in the morning to prepare the sourdough for bread and yeast dough for apple and plum cakes.

"Someday we'll have raisins on our apple cake again," Oma Anna would say, smiling.

But for Christine there was nothing in this world that could compare with Oma's freshly baked rye bread, baked in the glowing ashes of the stone baking oven, and eaten with freshly churned butter, prepared by Grandfather early Saturday morning. Churning butter was forbidden by tight government controls. So the farmers did it in secret.

"I don't care what the government tells me to do." Grandfather drew on his pipe. "We are doing the hard work and I don't feel a bit guilty." He paused. "My friend up there"—he pointed with his pipe towards heaven—"he knows what I am talking about. He is on my side."

One Saturday afternoon Oma Anna said:

"Christine, you have been here over a month now, and you haven't been to the Saturday night dance once. Young people must enjoy themselves. Life will be serious enough later."

As dusk settled over the village, Christine left for the dance hall less than ten minutes away. She could hear the trumpets and drums long before she opened the front door. More young people were heading towards the dance hall, the village *Gasthaus*. The air was chilly and damp. Christine wore her windbreaker over the white knitted cotton sweater, white knee socks, wooden shoes and the blue homespun skirt given to her by Mrs. Kohler.

A few people, mostly women, were dancing to the tunes of Glenn Miller's "In the Mood," and "A String of Pearls." But most people stood around watching the dancers and talking. Christine remained at the entrance, not sure whether she should stay. She moved further inside as more young people pressed from the door. A group of Russian soldiers appeared in the entrance, their weapons slung over their shoulders. The four windows on the opposite side of the entrance were wide open despite the chilly temperatures. It must have been from there that the sounds of the music had carried outside and could be heard throughout the village. A group of young men had assembled under the open windows.

Hella Schulz, accompanied by two other girls, waved, as the three made their way through the crowd towards Christine.

"You have finally come, Christine," Hella said. "These are my two cousins, Gudrun and Sylvia. They have just come from East Prussia. They are going to live with us for a while, until their parents arrive here. Their parents didn't want to leave their animals behind. They wanted to see what's going to happen to their home. People say that area will become Polish, *Pomorze,* they say, but that doesn't make sense. That area is all German."

They all nodded and shook hands. Gudrun, with her long blonde braids and soft blue eyes, could have been Hella's sister, she resembled her so much. Sylvia, the younger of the two, had a ruddy complexion, auburn hair, and lively green eyes. They looked around for a place where they would be less disturbed by people pushing in and out of the dance hall.

"It's going to happen again," Hella whispered, tapping Christine on the shoulder. She motioned towards the Russians by the door and the young men underneath the windows. "The boys over there are from the west, and the Russians know it."

"As long as the Russians keep their guns on their backs, it's all right; they're just watching."

The young men looked over at the girls. Three of them came over. The girls looked down demurely as the young men approached.

"They just can't help it," Hella murmured. "They always take chances, just to tease the Russians."

"May I have this dance, please?" A young man with blue eyes under a full head of neatly combed blond hair, with a deep melodious voice, swept Christine away even before he placed his arm around her. Without speaking they danced to the melody of "La Paloma."

"You must be new here," the deep voice finally said. "I've never seen you here. By the way, my name is Karl-Heinz Hoffmann."

They exchanged information about each other, but Karl-Heinz' eyes were most of the time on the Russians by the entrance.

"I'm from across the border," he whispered. "I must be careful."

They danced every dance together, sometimes talking, or just listening to the soft music and enjoying being with each other.

The band was taking a break and from the record player came a soft voice, singing: "J'attendrais, le jour et la nuit,-" (I'll wait for you, day and night—.)

The Russian soldiers by the entrance stepped outside and shot into the air. The dancers scrambled off the dance floor and towards the door. Karl-Heinz and others jumped out of the window. The Russians ran to the window and fired into the dark night. Screaming people pressed out of the door. Some threw themselves on the ground or crawled under the benches lined up by the wall.

"Let's go . . . let's go!" Hella grabbed Christine and Gudrun by the arm. Sylvia clung to Hella's skirt, shaking violently as they pushed each other out the front door. They ran across the street to hide behind a house. From there they could watch without being seen. The sounds of men's voices shouting and running had faded and were now far away.

"Let's see if they got away, otherwise the Russians will bring them to the *Kommandatura,*" Hella whispered. "This is the third time this has happened. The boys, ours and the Russian soldiers, simply enjoy this game. Nobody ever gets hurt."

In the darkness they listened and felt the silent presence of people hiding.

The music had stopped. The last people were coming out of the dance hall. A key was turned in the door. The lights went out.

"We'll take you home, Christine," Hella said after a while. "Now it is safe. The Russians are busy out there. And don't worry, those boys are all right. They've crossed by now. They've done it so many times. They'll probably be back next weekend."

Christine could not sleep for a long time. The excitement of her first "real" dance was overwhelming. The shooting had left her shaking for a long time, but she was still glad Oma Anna had sent her to the dance. She felt alive. She tried to imagine his face, and remembered exactly what he had said . . . the sound of his voice, and his smile. Perhaps she would see him again next Saturday, and the next, and the next.

The village of Rebenau is so small it can only be found on local maps. Up to July 3, 1945, it was one of more than a hundred small farm communities in Lower Saxony, hardly distinguishable from one another, with the largest city, Magdeburg, more than 150 kilometers to the south, and Berlin about 300 kilometers to the east. Inexplicably, the Allied powers had decided that the border between East and West Germany should run through the fields of this little village.

The border between the British and Russian Zones was never considered a permanent solution by the local people. There were, at that time, no fortifications, no barbed wire fences to make crossings impossible, no mines, no electric or electronic devices, as there were later. Only occasional wooden signs, painted white, with black lettering, reminded the people that they must go no further. Few middle-aged or older people ventured across "illegally," but the young people from both sides quickly found ways to sneak across, mainly on Saturday night for the dances. Russian soldiers and German border guards kept a 24-hour watch by walking an established beat. To avoid confrontation, contact between the farmers and the occupiers was kept to a minimum. The smartly dressed Russian officers were occasionally seen walking through the village. They kept a close eye on their soldiers. Some young German women tried to get the officers' attention, but soon it became clear to everyone that the Russian brass was not about to fraternize.

The local people had never been interested in politics. The only place where politics were discussed was at the local *Gasthaus* during the Saturday night card games over a glass of beer or a cognac in one of the backrooms. All important issues concerning the farmers of Rebenau had always been decided at higher levels and passed down from Wiedenbeck.

One day Grandfather was notified that his fields in the "*Birkengrund,*" the birch tree valley, now in the British Zone, would henceforth be tended by farmers from "over there," the west, while the fields formerly belonging to farmers in the west would be distributed to the farmers in the east. Grandfather shook his head and grinned.

"After all, the foreign powers have won the war," he said. "Let them have their fun for a while!"

He still thought it was all a silly game when, a year later, the tracks of the only railway leading to north-west Germany were blocked off by concrete slabs and barbed wire. But when, after another six months, the tracks were dismantled and taken away, he brooded more frequently and much longer than before over his cup of peppermint tea. Sundays he would spend the day on the large tree stump in the woods behind the barn. No one dared disturb him then, not even Oma Anna.

In the enjoyment of harvesting for the first time in years without the interruption from air alerts, the rumbling of distant artillery fire, or attacks by low-flying enemy planes, most of the farmers of Rebenau and other surrounding villages did not realize that they were gradually and systematically being cut off from the outside world.

Chapter 15

Heavy dark clouds drifted across the gray October sky. The howling storm tore leaves and branches from the trees, carrying dusty soil across the plain. Christine struggled against the gusty wind on her way to school. Often she had to dismount her bicycle, walking with it for long stretches, with the biting cold cutting through her worn clothing. She tried to suppress the tears clouding her burning eyes. Young Russian soldiers on horse drawn wagons and armored vehicles stopped, offering her a lift, but she shook her head and pushed on. The soldiers laughed as they drove away. Every afternoon she dropped her school bag on her bed and rushed out to the field to help harvest the sugar beets and potatoes, since, once the autumn rains started, they would last for days, or even weeks.

Winter arrived early. The rain turned to sleet and snow. Often Christine started out in the cold and dark morning, but because of the icy road conditions she had to turn back many times. Grandfather decided she should find a room in the city for the winter. She could come home on weekends and fill up on food to last her for a week.

The schools were not heated, no fuel was expected throughout the winter. Many children missed school. Those attending crouched on their benches with their coats and hats on, several pairs of socks on their feet. Half the class wore the *Knobelbecher*, the German military boot. Others wore the heavy felt boots designed for the Russian winter campaign. The students wore mittens in class, taking them off only to write, blowing into their hands to keep them warm.

On the school bulletin board Christine found the address of a couple who offered to take in students. She went there after school. She looked at the piece of paper on which she had scribbled the address: Hartmann, *Bismarckstrasse* 15.

Loud barking of dogs answered her knock on the door of the white-washed house. A short woman, perhaps in her forties, with blond braids around her head, opened the door a slit, trying to restrain two large dogs pressing out of the door. She listened for a moment, and said:

"Yes, I am *Frau* Hartmann. Let me get the dogs out of the way. I'll be right back."

Christine looked around. The house stood on a quiet suburban street. There were about ten of the same kind, single-family two story dwellings, with flower gardens in front, surrounded by boxwood hedges, and small wire-fenced yards with vegetable gardens and chicken coups in the back.

Mrs. Hartmann led Christine into the foyer, pointing to a rubber mat by the door on which Christine wiped her feet slightly longer than necessary. The foyer, connected to a hallway, was tastefully furnished with a small highly polished lady writing desk, and a round table with a white tablecloth embroidered in cross-stitch with coral-colored roses. A round crystal vase, filled with pine branches, stood in the center of the table. Four dainty chairs with needlepoint covers were arranged around the table, and Christine wondered if they were strong enough to even hold a child. How nice it would be if she could comment intelligently on the furniture style, only she had never been interested in such things. The parquet floor area not covered by Persian rugs showed accumulations of black and white dog hair. Bones and rubber toys were strewn about the rugs and on the bare floor.

Christine followed Mrs. Hartmann through the hallway into the living room. Mrs. Hartmann directed Christine to a large beige overstuffed chair. Christine sank into it, wondering how she might get out of it later in the most graceful way.

Mrs. Hartmann asked questions about Christine's family, about school, her grades, interests and hobbies. Christine tried to answer all questions. When Mrs. Hartmann asked about her life goal, Christine said:

"I want to become an interpreter or a teacher of foreign languages."

Frau Hartmann nodded her approval.

"My father was a professor of languages and linguistics at the Humboldt University in Berlin until he became the director of the Albrecht Gymnasium here," she said. "Unfortunately, I didn't inherit his talents." Smiling, she continued telling Christine about her husband, who was out at the moment, and who had been a major in the German army, in charge of the Subsistence Supply Section of the air base in Wiedenbeck since losing his right arm during the early war days in Poland in 1939. They had no children, and, all through the war, had taken in youngsters from large cities, bombed out areas, and later, refugee children from the east. In a few days they would give shelter to two little boys, brothers, three and five years old. They had lost their parents during a trek from East Prussia.

When Christine left less than an hour later it had been decided that she could move in at the end of November, less than ten days away, and that she would pay sixty Deutschmarks a month. She would be part of the family, a "house daughter," with all the duties and privileges of a family member. And, of course, they would "treat her the way her parents expected her to be treated." Further details could be discussed later, but Mrs. Hartmann was confident that they would have a good relationship.

"Now I would like for you to meet our dogs," Mrs. Hartmann said, getting up. She opened the basement door and two large, excited St. Bernard dogs came puffing up the stairs and started sniffing Christine's clothes.

"This is Senta, and this is Asta, her daughter," Mrs. Hartmann said. "They are friendly and you will have no problems with them." After a moment she sent the dogs downstairs, and walked Christine to the door. They shook hands and said goodbye.

"I'll have your room ready at the end of the month," Mrs. Hartmann said, closing the door behind Christine.

On her way back to the school, where she had left her bicycle, Christine noticed a sign in a window: Knitters wanted.

She stepped inside.

"I am moving to this area in two weeks and would like to work for you then."

"Sure," the woman behind the counter said. "We always have a lot of customers, mainly Russian women. They bring the yarn, we measure them, and they usually want the sweater in a week. Can you do that?"

Christine nodded. She would do anything to make it work. She needed the money, but she would never ask Grandfather.

Christine knew she would miss the evenings at the Lahrssen home, especially the bench by the warm tile stove in the living room. There was often no electricity for hours. Candles, made from animal fat, and smelly kerosene lamps, were the only source of light.

For the past weeks, Oma Anna, Christine and two refugee women who lived across the street, known as Zoya and her mother Bubbeh, had been spinning the greasy brown-beige sheep wool. Specks of wool and dirt, fall-out from the wool during the spinning, had to be swept away several times a day. Grandfather sat on the oven bench, his back on the warm tiles, listening to the whirring of the spinning wheels, smoking his pipe and keeping an eye on the apples baking in the oven. The bricks for the beds were warming in the upper part of the oven, and the sweet aroma of the baking apples mixed with the strong smell of Grandfather's tobacco. Of course, no one would dare to comment negatively on Grandfather's pipe smell. He was proud of his tobacco mixture, which he called the "Lahrssen Brand," a combination of American Chesterfield cigarette tobacco—provided by a neighbor, Mr. Holle, who regularly went to the American Zone—and the crude and strongly aromatic Russian *Makhorka*. For special occasions, Grandfather would add more Chesterfield tobacco to the mixture. Many evenings, Mr. Holle came by, carrying a decanter of his home-made schnapps. As a result, he and Grandfather often talked and argued about the state of the world into the early morning hours. Mr. Holle never worried about the curfew; he just sneaked back home through the woods. The Russians never caught him.

Mr. Holle talked about the first post-war German newspaper, the *Neue Zeitung,* now being published in the American Zone. It was hard to get it in the Russian Zone, but, once in a while, Mr. Holle managed to buy a copy on the black market.

"Now we learn what really happened in the Third Reich that we didn't know about." Mr. Holle said.

The war crimes trials in Nuremberg were to begin on November 25 and would probably be covered extensively by the *Neue Zeitung.*

"No matter, how guilty those people are," Mr. Holle said at one point. "The foreign powers have no right to sit in judgment over our leaders. That's a matter for the German people to deal with."

"I just hope, they don't make martyrs out of them," Grandfather said. "There are still plenty of people around for whom Hitler was a hero." He shook his head.

"Maybe the truth will finally come out."

At school in Wiedenbeck the Nuremberg trials were rarely mentioned. There it was a time of celebration. It was the 28th anniversary of the Communist October Revolution. The pictures of Karl Marx, Vladimir Ilyhich Lenin, and Josef Stalin were decorated with red banners. The students looked stoically at the portraits as Miss Olsheimer attempted to start another class in German history.

"November has often been a tragic month in the history of Germany," Miss Olsheimer began. "Just as a historical statement, the ninth of November comes to mind, when the *Fuhrer* lost sixteen of his most faithful followers in front of the *Feldherrnhalle* in Munich. And now we have the trials in Nuremberg."

The students gasped. Why was she doing this? Had she lost her mind? This was true Nazi propaganda! They looked at each other. Rosemarie von Hartenstein raised her hand.

"I think we have heard enough of that. Now we should really be informed about the new era, about the October Revolution, the causes, the events, and what it means to us. Can you tell us something about that, Miss Olsheimer?"

Rosemarie looked around with a victorious smile. All eyes were on her and on Miss Olsheimer who was desperately searching for a response to Rosemarie's impertinence. Miss Olsheimer knew that most students had no use for the new regime, so she could easily brush over this unfortunate incident with an admittance that she didn't really care for the Russians. With a strained smile she said into the tension-filled atmosphere:

"Honestly, I really can't. I haven't studied that yet, besides . . ."

"If you cannot teach us that, Miss Olsheimer, we must get another teacher!" Rosemarie shouted, jumping up. Without looking back she stalked out of the classroom, slamming the door.

The students did not move. They knew Rosemarie was not at all interested in learning about the Russian Revolution. She hated the Russians and talked openly against them, always saying that they were just as bad as the Nazis. Miss Olsheimer was nervously pacing back and forth, all the students' eyes upon her. Nobody had ever dared to talk to a teacher disrespectfully, much less leaving the classroom in that manner.

Rosemarie returned quickly with the principal, Dr. Steiner, accompanied by an unknown man. Dr. Steiner introduced the man as Dr. Nolte, a political officer. Dr. Nolte asked Rosemarie to repeat what had happened and then asked the class if they had witnessed the exchange. The students nodded in silence. The men talked briefly to Miss Olsheimer and Dr. Steiner and Miss Olsheimer left the classroom. Dr. Nolte proceeded immediately to draw a diagram on the blackboard to show the development of Communism and the advantages of the Communist system. He talked about Karl Marx, Lenin, Stalin, and especially about the Russian Revolution. He talked about the overwhelming task confronting the German people. The Free German Youth, especially the bright and educated ones before him, must work hard for a truly democratic state.

Dr. Steiner returned briefly and picked up Miss Olsheimer's handbag, coat and hat. She never came back. Dr. Nolte continued to teach history, especially Communist history, his specialty, until a suitable teacher was found a few weeks later.

Christine thought about the events of the day as she rode home that cold, wet afternoon. In the evening, during supper, she asked Grandfather:

"This new freedom everyone is talking about, Free German Youth, a Free Germany, I can't understand it. Today in history class, I looked at all those portraits of Marx, Lenin, and Stalin, decorated in red. It reminded me so much of the Third Reich, just the faces and flags were different." She searched Grandfather's eyes. When he did not answer, she spoke again:

"To me, it really is the same, only different faces in the frames, with different ideas, but, basically, it feels the same, don't you agree? Freedom, every second word is freedom.

What kind of freedom are they talking about? I certainly don't feel that freedom."

"Freedom from Fascism . . . that's all," Grandfather said simply.

Chapter 16

Limited mail service had resumed. Soon people knew that the Russian Zone was set apart from the three western zones, now called Tri-zone. Over there people could travel freely from one zone to another. To travel legally west from the Russian Zone, or Eastern Zone, *Ostzone* as it was called, was complicated by lengthy paperwork. To cross illegally was downright dangerous because the guards carried weapons and could use them at will. Radio communication was limited since electricity was often cut off for hours. When it was on, the radio disseminated local instructions and information, basically intended to "re-educate the German people that had been led astray by Hitler and his criminals."

Christine received her first letter from home. Harald informed her that there had been no word from Papa, but Mr. Brinkmann, the local butcher, had just returned from a French prisoner-of-war camp near Bad Kreuznach, not far from the Rhine crossing at Mainz. Mr. Brinkmann insisted that he had talked to Papa in the POW enclosure. He said that there were at least 35,000 Germans, Hungarians, and other Axis prisoners in an area of about half a square mile. He described in detail how the prisoners slept on the bare ground and that "people died like flies." They were just lucky that the weather had held up, otherwise few would survive. Being a POW of the French and their African troops was almost as bad as being with the Russians, he had said.

"If that was indeed your father, and I am confident that it was, he won't make it. He was too far gone."

But Harald assured Christine that Papa was strong and that one should not believe rumors so quickly. He went on to say that Mother was coming north a week before Christmas to see her parents and to take Christine home. Christine was sure that Mother's real reason for coming was to get food, since two people could carry more than one person.

On Saturday, December 1, Grandfather readied the wagon in the afternoon for the trip to Wiedenbeck. Christine felt good in her new sheep wool sweater, scarf, hat and mittens. She embraced Oma Anna quickly and climbed up on the seat next to Grandfather.

The wagon hobbled along the frozen tracks other vehicles had made in the snow. Deep deer tracks and soft footprints made by hares had painted a criss-cross pattern on the otherwise perfect snow blanket covering the fields on both sides of the road. The wind had shaken the snow off the crowns of the tall pine trees, but the small trees and bushes were still white with frozen snow. The air was crisp and fresh. Christine noticed tiny icicles forming on Grandfather's mustache. Grandfather pointed to a perfectly formed fir tree covered with snow.

"You see, Christine," he said. "This is the perfect Christmas tree. Once people get their hands on it, it has lost the touch of God."

They drove along in silence for a long time. When they arrived at the Hartmann house, Christine stepped from the wagon and picked up her few belongings from the back. Grandfather stayed up on his seat and drove off after waving briefly at Christine.

Christine, her parcel with the books in one hand, in the other the cardboard suitcase with her few clothes, walked slowly into the front gate of *Bismarckstrasse* 15. Tomorrow would be the first Advent Sunday. Soon it would be Christmas Eve, and, again, people all over the world, would pray for Peace on Earth.

Mrs. Hartmann answered Christine's knock on the door. Christine inhaled the fragrance of the advent wreath, made from freshly cut pine, which hung above the round table in the foyer, fastened to the ceiling by a hook with four wide red ribbons. The silver tinsels, carefully draped over the wreath, were wrinkled from repeated use. Slightly wider than the regular Christmas "lametta" icicles, they were probably the remnants of the aluminum strips Allied flyers had dropped to confuse the German anti-aircraft radar. Christine, in her mind, could still hear the sizzling sounds those strips made when they tumbled from the night sky in the outskirts of Magdeburg just before an air attack. And the next morning the school children had to gather them, roll them into balls, and turn them in to be used in the war industry.

Mr. Hartmann appeared from the hall and shook Christine's hand briefly with a slight bow.

"I see you like our advent wreath," he said. He was a tall thin man with dark-brown wavy hair and steel-gray eyes with only a slight touch of warmth.

Christine nodded.

"My wife just finished it this morning," he added, glancing at Mrs. Hartmann, standing by his side, smiling proudly.

"Well, let me show you to your room, Christine," Mrs. Hartmann suggested, still smiling. She picked up the battered suitcase and started up the stairs. Mr. Hartmann returned to his library adjacent to the living room.

"I hear the dogs scratching on the cellar door," Mrs. Hartmann called to her husband. "Don't let them in yet. They are too wet."

Removing her shoes at the bottom of the stairs, Christine followed Mrs. Hartmann. The polished steps were covered with a burgundy-colored runner with a Persian motif picturing, Mrs. Hartmann explained, repetitions of "Allah is the Only Victor," ending in front of Christine's room. An old chest of drawers, a night table, a dark-brown rocking chair with a large white hand-knitted afghan, and a high bed with thick down pillows, made the room look small and crowded. A framed print of Albrecht Durer's *Praying Hands* was the only decoration on the off-white wall. Christine walked up to the large picture window and looked at the snow-covered roofs in the distance.

"On days when the wind is right you can hear the sound of the bells of St. Mary's every half hour," Mrs. Hartmann said, adjusting the cushions on the bed. She turned the knob on the large radiator, "just to take the edge off the cold." The steam entered with a loud clanking sound that diminished after a while.

"We always turn the heat off at night," she said. "It's healthier to sleep in a cold room."

They left Christine's room and Mrs. Hartmann showed Christine the rest of the upstairs, the bathroom, the Hartmann's bedroom, and another bedroom larger than

Christine's that had been readied for the two little boys from East Prussia.

"We had the children for just a few days," Mrs. Hartmann explained. "We had to take them back. The younger one, Horst, three years old, cried constantly and Dieter, two years older, just sat with his arm around his brother all day, staring into the distance. They refused to eat. We tried everything, from bribing to punishing them. When nothing helped we decided those children needed more than we could provide."

She looked thoughtful, shrugging her shoulders.

"We did everything we could," she said.

"Now let's go downstairs," Mrs. Hartmann said. "I have some nice surprises for you."

Mrs. Hartmann had not wasted any time while waiting for Christine to arrive. Now in the living room, she told Christine that she had registered her in the church choir, but, unfortunately, Christine could not participate until after New Year's. The Christmas program had progressed to the point where they could not take any newcomers.

Christine nodded. She was not really interested in singing in the church choir.

"And here is another surprise," announced Mrs. Hartmann, showing large dimples as she smiled. "My friend Elsie, we went to school together, is a fine piano teacher. She is willing to teach you—only classical music, of course."

"Yes, I'd like that very much, thank you," Christine replied with enthusiasm.

"You see, your 60 marks will be well spent," Mrs. Hartmann spoke again. "We are not in this for the money. It is our genuine concern for young people who need help."

She moved to the coffee table and said:

"And here is something very special. You'll be part of the poetry recital group. I've been a member almost all my life. It's not easy to get in there—a very elite society." She smiled as she handed Christine the booklet. "You see you start out with something simple like this."

Christine started to read the first poem:

"In May, in May, all cats are gray . . ."

Oh, God, no, she thought, but quickly realized she had no choice. She had to get through the winter and would do her best to keep Mrs. Hartmann happy.

"Look, and then you go on to more difficult parts, and then to the classical pieces. I still remember most of Shakespeare's Juliet. I recited it when I was your age. Of course, my parents started me very early."

Mr. Hartmann appeared from the library, walking toward the dining room which was connected to the living room by two large wooden sliding panels kept open.

"We met during that time, didn't we, Hans?"

Mr. Hartmann looked at the two absentmindedly, nodding. After a moment he said:

"Yes, yes, dear, I remember. Why don't you recite your favorite lines for us? Now, how did it go?"

Together they started:

"Farewell! God knows when we shall meet again."

Mrs. Hartmann stopped, and then, smiling demurely, stretching herself and adjusting a few strands of her hair at the back of her head, and clasping her hands, continued:

"I have a faint cold fear thrills through my veins, that almost—almost . . ."

"Go on, Rita, you know how it goes—almost . . ." Mr. Hartmann tried to help.

"I can't . . . I really can't . . . I . . . don't have the looks anymore."

Mr. Hartmann walked to the window and looked out into the distance. His wife got up and joined him, hooking her arm into his.

Christine, embarrassed, picked up the poetry pamphlet, pretending to read.

I don't want to be like this when I grow older, she thought. There was Mrs. Hartmann, mourning her youth with memories of poetry recitations and church choirs. Perhaps that's the price one pays for a comfortable life. And she heard Grandfather say: "There's a whole world out there for those willing to take a chance. Hold on to your dreams!"

She had missed so much by not meeting Grandfather earlier in her life.

"Well, let's have *Kaffee* and *Honigkuchen* (honey cake)!" Mrs. Hartmann tried to sound cheerful as she discreetly wiped a tear away.

The table for the afternoon coffee hour was set in the dining room, fine Meissen china in the Blue Onion design on white damask cloth. The exquisite family silver completed the setting.

Christine, trying to make conversation to ease the uncomfortable atmosphere, said:

` "My family hasn't dug up their china and silver. They don't think it is safe yet."

"We never buried our things," Mrs. Hartmann replied, as she placed a piece of cake on Christine's plate, using a silver filigree cake lifter with a handle designed like a long-stemmed rose. "Life is more bearable when you are surrounded by beautiful things."

Christine had to admit that the sticky, leaden cake tasted better because it was served in such an elegant way.

Mr. Hartmann was a quiet man who spent most of the day in his library. Mrs. Hartmann told Christine later that, before Christine arrived, he had left his house almost every day to find work, since his military pay had ceased at the end of the war. But Russian patrols, always checking German men in the hope of catching a Nazi or a member of the SS, had stopped him constantly, asking for *dokumyente*. Even though his papers were in order, the soldiers always dragged him along to the *Kommandantura*, keeping him there for several hours, until they would finally let him go home. Now he stayed inside most of the time, occupying himself with reading and learning to write with his left hand. The Hartmanns did not have to worry about food or money, even though their bank account, like everybody else's, had been "frozen" at the end of the war. They had many valuables they could trade in for food.

Every morning Christine left the house at 7:30 to be at the school at the first ringing, ten minutes to 8:00. After a few days she met a girl her age, walking the same route to school. From then on the girls waited for each other at the crossing *Bismarckstrasse* and *Strasse der Jugend*, newly named for the Free German Youth, replacing the old *Hindenburgstrasse*, to walk together. Inge Roloff lived with her mother in a rented room in an adjoining sub-division. Her father, a *Luftwaffe* pilot, had been shot down over Poland in the first days of the war. Inge's mother supported the two by taking in sewing. Two years before they had been bombed out in Duesseldorf and moved inland. They could have resettled to the west legally after the Russians arrived, but Inge's mother was tired of moving. Besides, she had accumulated a nice clientele.

One afternoon the two girls were walking along the Strasse der Einheit—the Avenue of Unity—past the Unity

Café, former City Café, across a narrow bridge over the Jeetze Canal. Christine stopped to look over the railing at the dilapidated houses bordering the muddy water, known as "Little Venice."

"Look at this, Inge, Little Venice! Someday I'll see the real Venice and I will gaze at the *Canale Grande* from the *Ponte Vecchio*, and I'll send you a postcard."

Inge looked at Christine. She burst out laughing.

"You are a dreamer, Christine!" She shook her head. "Life is not like that. Your life is here. You see . . ."

She pointed along the wide poplar-lined Avenue of Youth.

"If you walk straight along for five kilometers, you are in the west—if you don't get caught, which you probably will. But if not, the police from over there will send you right back, at the latest when it is time for new ration cards, because you are under age and your family is here." They started to walk.

"So, in no later than ten days, you'll be back where you started, and you'll be a 'marked woman,' a person "not to be trusted." No, Christine, in life you have to be realistic. You have to make plans that are within the range of possibility."

"What about your plans, Inge, have you made any? What are you going to do after you are finished with school?"

"I'll be a medical doctor someday," Inge said with determination. "You see, anyone can become a medical doctor now, if you work hard for it. We don't have to pay tuition anymore. Before, only the rich could study medicine. Now it's open to all of us."

They walked a while in silence, each occupied with her own thoughts.

"How can you get married and have children when you have so many years of studying before you?"

Inge shook her head.

"Not me . . . I'm not going to get married," she said. "Most of the boys of our generation are dead or crippled or missing. It will be a long time before even the healthy ones can think of raising a family and then . . . look at me! Do you think of those that are left even one would give me a second look? Men choose their partners with their eyes first."

Christine looked at the frail figure. A heavy brown coat was draped over thin shoulders, hanging loosely down to her ankles. Dull light blue eyes gazed at Christine from a grayish face surrounded by thin, straight, mousy hair, covered with a thick maroon-colored hat knitted from ersatz wool. The serious expression in the small face prevented Christine from saying something funny to ease the atmosphere.

"But you'll probably get married," Inge said simply.

"Oh, no!" Christine shook her head. "Even if someone would ask me, there are so many things I want to do first, and then it will be too late to raise a family. So, I'll do it the way you are doing it, make plans for myself first." She smiled and hooked her arm into Inge's. Together they continued their walk home.

` "I still might write you that postcard from Venice," Christine spoke again, more as a joke.

"Just be sure you address it to Dr. Inge Roloff," Inge countered in the same mood.

As they were passing the knitting store, Christine said:

"I'm going to work for them, but I don't want to go in now, maybe tomorrow afternoon."

"My mother worked for them for a while," Inge said. "She stopped after a month, there were too many problems. For example, one young Russian woman came in with the yarn, they measured her and started the sweater, and then another, a real heavy one, came to pick it up and wanted to try it on. So the employees had to stretch it with a steam iron in the back room. No, it's not worth it, too many problems, and they pay very little."

I won't worry about money at this time, Christine thought. The schools are open again and education must be my main focus. Everything else will fall into place.

Chapter 17

Christine's seventeenth birthday fell on the third Advent Sunday. Mrs. Hartmann lit three candles on the small advent wreath on the living room table. She handed Christine two flannel nightgowns that she had outgrown. She had sewn new, fresh looking lace around the collars and sleeves which made the gowns look almost new. She brought out a pair of leather boots, lined with lamb's wool, and told Christine to try them on. They fit and were added to the presents. Mr. Hartmann appeared from the library with a small volume of Goethe's "The Sorrows of Young Werther" and said:

"This is my present for you, Christine. Goethe, our greatest poet, represents the true Germany."

Christine took the little book, bound in soft red leather, with gold lettering. She instantly knew she would treasure it for the rest of her life.

"Life will not be easy for you as you go into the future," Mr. Hartmann spoke again. "It will be difficult to be true to yourself. People all over the world are throwing rocks at

Germany, accusing us of barbaric behavior and atrocities. I cannot believe those stories are true, German soldiers are not like that. But who are we to defend ourselves? We've lost the war. We have no voice."

He looked thoughtfully into the distance.

"But you and all the young people must remember the events of our recent past are only a phase in history. Our country has much to be proud of. Never forget, a Germany that produced a Himmler, Goebbels and Goering and the like, also gave the world men like Beethoven . . . whose birthday we also celebrate today"—he smiled but quickly turned serious again, " . . . and, of course, Goethe, Brahms, Bach, Handel, Martin Luther, Albert Einstein, and many other great people."

After a long silence, Christine asked:

"What would you do if you were my age?"

"I would try hard to do what my heart dictates. You see, we Germans know how to take orders. We respect, even fear authority. That's why everybody tries to get into a position where he can give orders and, hopefully, doesn't have to obey any. That's the life goal for most of our people. Put a man in uniform and he thinks he is God."

He lit his pipe with an advent candle.

"And the intellectuals, they are out of touch with reality. They live in their own world. They stay with their own kind and out of politics. For them politics is a 'dirty business' and beneath them." He mused. "It would be interesting to know how different the history of the world would have turned out had thinkers been the leaders of nations."

He paused and looked at Christine.

"But this can't possibly interest you. I always get carried away. I simply forgot that you are a girl, and girls like to talk about . . ."

"Oh, no," Christine interrupted. "All this interests me very much. I always wanted to discuss things like that with my father, but he never seemed to have the time. There's so much I want to know, and to learn, especially philosophy, psychology and history."

Mr. Hartmann smiled and said:

"Life experience helps to understand the philosophers better. I'll gladly try to answer any questions you might have. Just come and ask. You know where to find me."

Mrs. Hartmann glanced at her husband, happy that he had found a listener. For the first time in months he seemed alive.

In silence they watched the flickering lights of the burning candles. Dusk settled over the city. The soft lights of advent, the fragrance of the pine needles mixed with that of the burning candles, and the sound of the crackling wood fire in the tile stove, exuded a feeling of warmth and hope for a future no one could imagine. During supper the Hartmanns told Christine they would like it if she called them Uncle Hans and Aunt Rita. Christine was glad she had found a new home.

Christine had not returned to Rebenau since her arrival in Wiedenbeck. Cold temperatures, snow and icy roads, had kept her from undertaking the trip.

On Monday noon, Grandfather, on his errands in Wiedenbeck, waited outside the school in his sled to tell Christine that Mother would arrive in Wiedenbeck two days later. Since her arrival coincided with the last day of school, Christine should walk to the station in the afternoon to meet Mother. Grandfather would pick them both up and take them to Rebenau. He handed her an envelope brought to the house by a young man from the west, he said. The young man had been twice at the Lahrssen's house asking when '*Fräulein* Christine' might come to visit again. Christine stashed the unopened note into her coat pocket to open it as soon as she would be alone.

"I would like to see you again. Karl-Heinz," the note said. Christine felt her heart beating stronger as she read the lines. When she saw Inge coming across the street, she quickly pushed the note back into her pocket. Now she had a special secret, something nice to think about, too tender to share with anyone.

The next day Christine's class was ordered to meet a refugee train at the main station on its way to the west. The girls were to serve broth, tea and milk provided by the Red Cross. The freight train, loaded to bursting with old people, mothers and children, moved slowly into the station as soon as the school children arrived.

"Everybody move back from the edge!" the station master shouted as he and other railway officials rushed back and forth along the platform. The train stopped and the uniformed men opened the large sliding doors.

Rosemarie von Hartenstein and Christine were detailed together. Rosemarie moved her cart to the opening and started to ladle the liquids into metal cups for Christine to hand to the outstretched hands of the people huddling, body on body, on the straw-covered floor. The odor of unwashed bodies and human waste pressed out of the door.

Christine stared at a young woman with large blue eyes in a pale face. Her whole figure was enveloped in a black shawl and black clothing. She nervously pushed an infant away from her breast, buttoning up her dress, when she realized the door was being opened. The baby began to cry. Christine, a cup of hot broth in each hand, kept staring. A modern Madonna, she thought, Madonna of the Wars.

"What's the matter with that dumb girl, a woman shrieked. "She stands there with the drinks and stares. Hurry up, we're thirsty!"

"Someone else should do her job, something is wrong with her," another woman added.

Christine looked up, and started pushing the drinks into outstretched hands. The women returned the cups quickly to be refilled, handed out, and again refilled.

After the rush Christine handed another cup to the young woman, whispering:

"The people I'm living with, the Hartmanns, have a good home and they love children. They could take care of your baby. It is too cold out here. Your baby might—might die. And some day, when you have found a home, you could come and get your baby."

The woman looked at Christine with moist eyes. She could not be older than twenty, Christine thought.

"Oh, no, I could never give her up," the woman said softly. "She's all I have, she keeps me alive."

Christine glanced at a small pine tree tied to a nail above her.

"It's from home," the woman said. "Wherever we'll be when we arrive, I want her to have her first Christmas with a tree from our garden in Koenigsberg."

Christine nodded with tear-filled eyes.

"Everybody step back! The train is getting ready to leave!" The station master strode along the platform, waving his arms to make people move back. As the heavy door closed, the young woman lifted her small hand in a tired goodbye gesture.

"I waited for a whole hour with lunch for you," Aunt Rita said annoyed. "Everything is dried out now. You should tell me when you are late, Christine."

"I didn't know," Christine said in a tired voice. "We had to meet a refugee train. They just told us this morning. I'm sorry."

Aunt Rita left the dining room without a word. Christine walked up the stairs with a heavy heart, wondering who the victims of the war really were, those who had died or those who had survived.

"Your food is on the table," Aunt Rita called in an irritated voice. Christine was glad she was eating alone. Strange, she thought, we have just survived a war, many people are still suffering, and here is a person lucky enough to be spared all that misery, and she bickers about unimportant things. She shook her head.

On the last day of school Christine said goodbye to the Hartmanns in the afternoon to go home for the Christmas vacation. The train was just arriving from Magdeburg as she entered the platform. There was Mother. She seemed smaller than Christine remembered her, with a large kerchief around her head, wearing Papa's old coat which was much too large for her and had two buttons missing, so that she had to hold it closed with her hand. She had a rucksack strapped on her back and was carrying another rucksack in a large shopping net Christine had crocheted for her several Christmases before. The two embraced briefly. Christine took Mother's arm and steered her through the gray mass of people to the exit.

Grandfather stepped from the sled when he saw the two coming. He embraced Mother tenderly and, with great care, tucked them both into the blankets. Another large blanket was draped across and fastened at the sides of the sled.

Oma Anna had waited by the living room window. When she held her daughter whom she had not seen in over two years, they both wept quietly. Later, during supper, Christine noticed Mother savoring every bite of the potatoes dipped in the bacon and onion mixture. For once she could eat without having to worry whether there was enough food left for the rest of the family.

While Oma Anna and Mother were talking, Grandfather got up to bring the bedding from the guest room. He draped it over two chairs close to the tile stove and added two more bricks to the ones already in the oven shelves. Over peppermint tea and honey cake made with sugar syrup, the adults talked into the early morning hours. Christine slipped into her new flannel nightgown and snuggled into her warm bed to read her new Goethe volume. Her mind wandered to the woman on the train. How fortunate she herself was, to live such a comfortable life. And she was ashamed that she had almost forgotten how much misery there was.

Chapter 18

It had snowed again during the night. Large soft snowflakes were still falling when Oma Anna closed the heavy wooden gate behind Grandfather who was taking Mother and Christine to the station in Wiedenbeck to board the only train going south that day. The air was heavy with moisture. Judging from the low hanging sky there would be snow all day. The sled glided swiftly over the fresh snow on the almost deserted highway.

Christine felt content. Both rucksacks were filled with sugar, flour, rye grains, potatoes, butter, sugar beets, a smoked ham, and a goose, killed and plucked the night before. When they arrived at the station, Grandfather lifted the rucksacks on the women's backs and watched as the two, bending under the heavy load, joined the stream of travelers towards the entrance. Then he drove away.

The station in Wiedenbeck was a two-story brick house with three platforms for trains. In normal times it had been more than adequate, but since it was now a *Grenzstation*, with border traffic, and thousands of refugees moving back and forth, it was always crowded, even during the night.

Christine and Mother made their way through the people huddling on the floor. Most window openings were covered with cardboard and wooden boards, since the glass panes, shattered by artillery fire during the last days of the war, had not been replaced. The darkened light bulbs from the days of black-out kept the room in constant semi-darkness.

After mother bought Christine's ticket—Mother had a round-trip ticket from Bahrenberg—they moved to the third class waiting room. They removed their rucksacks and sat down at a square wooden table. They ordered two bouillons from the middle-aged waitress. The hot liquid made them forget the cold room for a while.

"How are things at school?" Mother asked, sipping the soothing liquid.

"Oh, wonderful, Mother, I am learning so much," Christine's voice was filled with excitement. "Last week we got a new English teacher. He just arrived from England."

"An Englishman?" Mother asked surprised. "Why would an Englishman come to Germany at this time?"

"Well, he is not really English," Christine replied. "He just lived in England since 1938. Before that he was a foreign language teacher at a boys' school in Dresden. But he had a problem with the Nazis and had to leave the country. He doesn't want to go back to Dresden. He says he is tired of seeing bombed out cities, it's too depressing."

She paused and then continued:

"You know, Mother, that's really fate. I have always wanted to learn English from someone who has lived in an English-speaking country, and there he is, Dr. Alfred Schwartz. And since I want to study many foreign languages, I talked to him about which author I should chose for my graduation paper. He said H.G. Wells would be a good choice, and he right away gave me some books to read."

Mother looked thoughtful. She did seem to share Christine's enthusiasm in her quiet way. She probably never heard of H.G. Wells, Christine decided, and she doesn't know what to say. And Christine went on talking about school in general, about the Hartmanns, and how she had learned that Mr. Vogel had been killed by the foreign laborers. Mother still did not say anything. She just nodded, sipping her drink.

Finally, she took a deep breath and said:

"Christine, there is something I must tell you. I had wanted to wait until we got home so Harald could be with us, but, well, you can't go back to school for a while. I've talked to Grandfather about it, and as soon as I let him know our final decision, he'll pick up your things from the Hartmanns."

Christine turned pale.

"But why?" she gasped.

"The mayor has told us that, since Papa was in the Nazi party, they have to find out first if he deserves to be paid full time and whether he'll be qualified to teach when he comes back. So they have stopped his pay. They call that a de-*Nazification* process. She sighed. "I know this is such a disappointment for you. We have tried everything. Harald has asked Mr. Alpert if he can use his influence, but there is nothing he can do. We just have to wait. We simply cannot afford the sixty marks for the Hartmanns and we need you to earn money. When Papa comes back, I am sure you can go back to school, but right now . . ."

She shook her head and added:

"I just don't know what else to do."

Christine could not speak. There was no use suggesting that perhaps Grandfather could pay until Papa returned. Borrowing money, even within the family, was the lowest one could fall. Christine's thoughts raced from the Hartmanns to Grandfather to school to Harald to Bahrenberg and to Hermann Bretten, the manager of the co-op store who wanted to marry her, and back to school and her life in Wiedenbeck. No, it could not end like this. She would have to talk to Harald during the Christmas holidays. Yes, she should earn money, but what could she do? Where could she find work? She had no skills, just school knowledge. And what if Papa returned and couldn't get his job back? She would end up in Bahrenberg, live for the rest of her life with shallow, boring, gossipy people, get married early and be an old woman at 35. No, she must talk to Harald. There must be a way, and together they had to find it.

Yes, she did understand Mother who had lived through two devastating wars, lost her father at the age of twelve in World War I, and had lived through the terrible depression. And now she was confronted with an uncertain future with four young children. All she wanted was a decent life for them all. For her it was enough that the war was over and they had survived it.

The door opened and a bulky official in a tight-fitting German army uniform shouted:

"The baggage control is now open!"

He quickly turned around, slamming the door from the inside.

The baggage control had been established to curb the influx of black market items from the west, especially American cigarettes, the most popular currency of the time.

Christine and Mother finished their bouillon. They helped each other with their rucksacks and lined up at the far end of the station hall.

"I really should get my hair cut," Christine moaned, trying to untangle her long braids that had gotten caught in the rucksack straps. Mother did not answer. She watched with mounting uneasiness as the middle-aged official brought out food and clothing items from suitcases, attaché cases, rucksacks, handbags and sacks. Russian soldiers, their weapons slung over their shoulders, stood by the wall, looking at the crowd with a bored expression. One soldier, stocky, with red hair and freckles, stood by the baggage table, watching the proceedings. He laughed when the official picked up a pair of panties and a black slip for the entertainment of everyone around.

"He must have been a cook in the army," Christine whispered. Mother nodded. She agreed that the rotund official must have been at the right place throughout the war.

"Let's see what we have here, little lady," the official sneered at Christine, opening her rucksack. He brought out the smoked ham.

"Confiscated," he shouted and threw the ham to his colleague. The second official placed the ham into a box under the table. Christine looked aghast. She hoped the whole scene was just a joke, but a look at the official's face told her he was serious.

"You know it's against regulations to carry such a large ham around when so many people are starving, don't you?" He brought out the remaining contents, potatoes, turnips, and sugar beets. "Do you know how many refugees we can feed with that ham? You didn't get that with you ration cards, did you now!"

"I did not get it on the black market," Christine said timidly. "I got it in the country."

"In the—country?" He pushed the vegetables back into the rucksack. "In the country!" he chuckled. "Looks like the quotas for the farmers need a little tightening!"

The primitive looking Russian soldier laughed, enjoying Christine's embarrassment. Christine doubted he even understood one word. Mother had watched the proceedings, suppressed anger on her face. She feared the official might take away everything if she said a word.

Christine had left the pillow case with the goose on the ground, pushing it past the table with her foot. The official began to open Mother's bag.

"What's that white thing down there?" barked the second official. "Put that on the table, but fast! What is it?"

"A goose," Christine whispered."

"A gooose?" the first official shouted in disbelief. "And you had forgotten that you had that, right? Else you would have presented it to me, of course."

He looked around for applause for his cruel joke, but the people watched in stony silence.

"Did you really think you could smuggle that through? Young lady, we've seen everything! Next time you won't be so lucky. I am nice today, because it is Christmas time."

He gave her a menacing look through his wire-rimmed glasses.

"I could have you arrested. You know that, don't you? Now I am a kind man, I know how it feels to be hungry, but in times like these we must not just think of ourselves, especially when there are so many hungry people out there. You should be ashamed!"

He grabbed the pillow case with the goose and said:

"Put that in the box with the ham, Fritz!"

Mother's hands were shaking as she pushed her rucksack towards the official. Pale, lifeless, she was holding on to the table while Christine was tying her rucksack. The official took out the butter and sugar, rye grains, apples and potatoes and spread them across the table. He threw the butter into the box with the ham, and stuffed the rest back into the rucksack without a word. He motioned with his hand for the women to move on to make room for the next person. Mother's whole body was shaking now. Christine held her arm as they slowly walked to the platform where the train was waiting.

"He even took the butter," she said, wiping her tears away with the back of her hand and shaking her head.

Christine thought of Uncle Hans' words, that being in power meant everything for the little man. She held Mother's arm as they moved towards the train. They found a compartment where all the window panes were intact. Christine helped Mother to climb the high steps. The compartment filled quickly while Christine sat down in the window seat opposite Mother. People were stashing their packages and sacks into the baggage rack above the seats and underneath, settling down for the journey that would last seven hours or more.

An old man, wearing a ragged army winter coat, sat down next to Christine. He smelled of a mixture of sweat, tobacco and onions. As the train began to move, he took a cigar box out of an olive-drab canvas bag, and placed it on his lap. It was filled with loose tobacco and a small cigarette machine. From his coat pocket he produced a package of cigarette paper and began to roll a cigarette. His hands trembled as he tried to keep the precious tobacco from spilling. Finally, he moistened the long side of the paper with his tongue and pressed it together. He lit the cigarette and offered it to Christine.

"Cigarette?"

Christine shook her head.

"Well, I should've known that girls like you don't have to smoke cigarettes made from cigarette butts, they can get Chesterfields and Lucky Strikes anytime, right?" He smiled a nasty smile.

"And chocolates, too, and silk stockings . . ." his voice became louder. He laughed, looking around for approval, but the other travelers stared impassively ahead.

"Shut up and leave the girl alone!" A young German soldier, still in his uniform, said gruffly.

"Did you hear that?" the man gasped. "This is what war does. It makes the young lose respect for their elders."

Again he tried to get the attention of the other passengers but without success.

"I told you to shut up!" the soldier spoke again, in a voice mixed with anger and fatigue. "And if you make one more sound I'll smash your face in. . . . makes me want to puke when I think that my friends died for scum like you."

The old man puffed on his cigarette, shrugging his shoulders.

Mother closed her eyes, leaning her head against the window frame as soon as they were settled. Christine looked out on the peaceful winter scene wondering what lay ahead.

An icy wind blew into the unheated compartment as the conductor and a young Russian soldier entered from the platform connecting the railway cars. The passengers fumbled for their tickets and identification cards.

"Tickets, please*! Documeyente, pashaluste* !"

The Russian soldier checked the ID cards, returning them almost immediately. He took Christine's card, looked at her, then at the card. He turned it around, inspecting it on both sides, again and again. Then, looking at her again, he said:

"*Nye khorosho,* no good!" He dropped the card into his uniform pocket and started to walk off.

"But why?" Christine burst out. "What's wrong with my card?"

"No good, I say, that's why," the Russian soldier shouted, angry because his actions were questioned. "When train stops you come with me to see Commandant!"

Christine began to tremble. Mother leaned over and whispered:

"Don't worry! I'll go with you. I am sure it is a mistake." She touched Christine's arm to calm her down. The old man grinned. It looked like he wanted to say something, but decided against it when he saw the soldier half getting up.

Another Russian soldier, tall and slightly older, came from the opposite side through the train, asking for ID cards. Christine pointed to the first one who was now half-way through the train.

"He has my card," she said timidly.

The second patrol turned around, shouting:

"*Misha . . . yedi syuda!*—Come here!"

The first soldier came back at once. They talked, pointing at Christine and at the card Misha had brought from his pocket. He pointed at the seal and they both studied it intensely. Their talk turned into an argument as they got more excited. Finally, the second soldier tore the card away from the first one, hit him with the back of his hand across the face and threw the card into Christine's lap.

"*Khorosho*—o.k.!" he snapped, his face red from the heated argument, "Mistake!"

A few hours later the train came to a halt in the main station of Stendal. Christine watched as the two Russians, gesticulating and laughing, strode toward the exit together.

Soon after the train left the station, the passengers dozed off, one by one, coming to life only when the train slowed down to enter the Magdeburg main station, where the train ended. Christine and Mother changed to the local crowded with working people going home. As the train approached Bahrenberg, Christine searched for members of her family. There was Harald, holding the rope of a sled. Manfred was sitting on the sled, wrapped up to his neck in an army blanket, his head covered with a knitted hat. When Harald saw Mother, he knew. He placed his arm around her shoulders as she told him what had happened.

"Pigs!" Harald said disgusted. "We all know where the confiscated ham and goose will go. Into their stomachs, that's where! They don't turn that stuff in, everybody knows that!"

Christine took the rope out of Harald's hand to pull the sled.

"Faster, faster!" Manfred shouted as Christine ran through the snow. It was bliss to be home again.

Chapter 19

hristmas Eve 1945 was a clear and sunny day. The snow had lost its whiteness. The horse and wagon tracks, frozen now, had formed a bumpy surface difficult to walk on. The icy north wind prevented the noon sun from melting any of the week-old snow, blown into drifts on *Breite Strasse*. The drab looking houses showed no signs of life, the streets were deserted. No one ventured out into the cold. It was difficult to get warmed up afterwards since the only place where a fire was lit was the kitchen stove, and that only when used for cooking.

Mother and Christine searched in the closets for clothes to wear for the Christmas Eve church service.

Christine held up Manfred's trousers, worn thin at the knees. Manfred was wearing Gerhard's jacket, with sleeves much too long, and put on his own pants, with legs much to short. Christine tried to find a pair of socks that would cover the bare skin from the edge of his oversized shoes to the seams of his trousers. She looked at him. His pale face looked even whiter and smaller in his black outfit. He smiled.

"It fits!" He beamed, looking down and running his little hands along his sides. "Fits just right, doesn't it, Christine?"

"Yes," Christine replied. "You look very handsome."

Manfred walked away, still stroking his jacket.

"In the west people can get clothing now on their ration cards," Christine said.

"That doesn't help us any," Harald snapped. "The west-the west-that's all we hear from you anymore, Christine."

"It's true, Christine, you make it sound like a paradise," Mother said. "People have to struggle there, too. Everything takes time. Things are improving here also." Christine felt the anger welling up in her.

"It's alright to wait for clothing and for food, but can't you see? These people are talking about helping Germany to recover, and at the same time they carry whole factories off to Russia." Christine screamed. "They are talking about freedom while they are locking us in. They try to keep us ignorant and uninformed, just like our former government. My God, what does it take to make you see what's going on?" Her voice was trembling, her eyes burning.

"Shhh, Christine!" Mother rushed over. "Do you want us all to end up in jail?"

"You see? We are already afraid. Just like before. It's the same—the same!"

Harald jumped up and ran to the door, opening it slightly. He looked around and quietly closed it again. He had to admit, Christine was right. But what could they do? Wasn't it enough that he was taking care of the family? There was much under the new regime he didn't agree with, but considering the total destruction at the end of the war, the daily life of the people was improving. But Christine's outbursts, especially in front of the younger children, could not be tolerated.

"I don't know what's wrong with you, Christine. You have changed. Maybe being away from home has gone to your head. You are surrounded by the wrong people." He took a deep breath.

"I am trying to make a new life here for all of us, and comments like yours can be disastrous for us. We are being watched all the time. It simply is not easy for the new government to start Germany in a new direction, and they just have to be suspicious for a while."

He walked to the window and looked at the snow-covered roofs glistening in the setting sun. The sound of Christmas melodies emanated from the *Volksempfaenger* radio, one of the legacies of the Third Reich.

"This is not a time for adventure, but for clear thinking and patience," he said, still looking out of the window.

"I understand," Christine mumbled. But she didn't. What had happened to Harald? What had happened to his spirit to reach high? Had the few months during the war crushed them? Or was it the responsibility of being the head of the family? Would he ever be his real self again when things became more normal? Or was he, without realizing it, on the same path Papa and so many others had been only a short while ago? And she thought of the earlier days when she and Harald, in their secret place, had discussed the happenings of the time, criticizing the adults who had lived for so long in a strained and fearful atmosphere without doing anything about it, that it had become an accepted way of life.

She felt confused and terribly alone. Her life was crumbling away. The only person who had understood her had deserted her. She did not fit in anymore, but how could she give up her ideals, abandon her principles? She instantly realized that, if she went against the grain, she must take responsibility for her actions and face the consequences. She must speak to Harald. The world out there looked very frightening, but to live here?

At the onset of darkness the Bachmanns, dressed in their best clothes, their feet crunching on the frozen snow, joined the stream of worshippers summoned by the church bell to celebrate the birth of Christ. Harald walked in front, Ulrich and Gerhard walked with Manfred in their midst, and behind them, their woolen shawls drawn over their faces to shield them from the biting wind, walked Mother, Christine and Ruth. The sky sparkled with stars, a perfect night for an air raid had the war still been on. Yes, there was something to be thankful for, even if God did not always work as hard as He should.

Pastor Konrad Wenzel, who had come as a refugee from Danzig, now Polish territory, lit the candles on the altar and on the Christmas tree. He strode along the aisle, welcoming his flock with a smile, happy that the people were finally finding their way back to God. In times like these it was not easy to keep the faith. He walked towards the Bachmanns with outstretched arms.

"There's a member of the family I haven't met yet," he exclaimed. His sparkling, youthful eyes stood in stark contrast to his full head of white hair.

"Welcome!" He grasped Christine's hand and then reached left and right to shake hands with other members of the family. He hurried to greet others, casting a suspicious glance at the Russian soldiers milling by the entrance.

As the organist played softly the age old melodies of Christmas, the school children lined up next to the organ to sing at their appointed time. And when Pastor Wenzel, in his deep baritone voice, recited the Christmas story, that every child and adult knew by heart, the congregants felt a bond they had not known for a long time. The song of Silent Night, Holy Night, sung by the children and picked up by the congregation, signaled the end of the service. Pastor Wenzel blessed his parishioners and the shivering people rushed out of the cold church to their sparsely heated homes.

Harold lit the fire in the living room stove. For the last time the four advent candles, burned down to a stump, were lit. Mother watched closely that the fire would not ignite the dried out pine needles that had little fragrance left. The eight brown-coal briquettes, neatly stacked by the stove, received a surprise look from the rest of the family, since they had become a rarity, but no questions were asked. Neither did Harald reveal that Heinz Sudermann, the baker's son and Harald's army buddy, had, "by depriving the economy of essential fuel, an act of sabotage," enhanced the spirit of Christmas in the Bachmann home. The family, enjoying the cozy fire and soft candle light, gathered around the piano as Christine began to play the old Christmas melodies.

Soon Mother tucked the younger children into bed and not long thereafter Ulrich and Gerhard went to their beds so they could be up at dawn. Mother cast a final glance into the "Christmas Room," pleased about the abundance of gifts. There were mufflers, socks, mittens, and hats knit from Oma Anna's sheep wool, coasters and table mats made from wooden beads, card games, picture frames and portfolios made from colorful poster board. There were necklaces for the girls made with tiny glass beads, a doll for Ruth, sewn from bed sheet scraps and stuffed with kapok, a fluffy gray mass. She arranged the wooden train Harald had built for Manfred during many long fall and winter nights.

Yes, there was much to be thankful for. The guns had stopped, no more air alerts, and, according to the radio announcer, the whole world was, again, trying to work towards eternal peace.

After Mother had gone to bed, Harald put one more coal briquette on the dying fire. He went to the cabinet and brought out a bottle of Russian vodka. He filled a small tumbler and offered some to Christine. She shook her head.

"*Na starovye!*" Harald said, lifting his glass. "*Prosit!* Let's be friends again, Christine!"

"*Prosit*—to a good life!" Christine said, lifting her tea cup.

Harald gulped down the vodka.

"I don't want you to misunderstand me, Christine," Harald began. "But I have seen what happens to people if they go against the system. No matter how young or how old you are, if you have no power, you are nothing. You might get angry and even pay for your anger with your life, but nothing is accomplished."

"It's all right!" Christine motioned with her hand that she considered the discussion unnecessary. Politics did not interest her. She judged by what she saw.

Harald poured himself another drink, and said:

"We are all influenced by our experiences and don't believe anymore everything people tell us. We young people feel utterly betrayed. Perhaps each of us must now find his or her own way, do what we feel is right for us. But for the sake of the family, whatever you do, I don't want to know about it. I want to always be able, if questioned under pressure, to insist that I didn't know anything. It is most important that you don't entrust your secrets to anyone,

anyone at all! Those who love you will always respect your actions, and—forget about the others."

His face was grave as he looked at Christine for a long time. They watched the glowing fire and did not speak. Christine got up and filled her cup with the now cold and strong tea. She returned and said:

"Harald, I wish you would convince Mother to let me return to school for this semester. No secretarial school will accept me at this time, and, if I stayed home, all the time would be wasted, even though I would enjoy being with all of you. But I need more education and really want to graduate.

Harald knew that all Christine wanted was to go north, to cross the border and find out what the west was all about. Once she got stuck in Bahrenberg, she had no chance of leaving. The border was too far away. With the trace of a smile he said:

"I guess we could manage that, Christine, but it would help if you could find some kind of work in Wiedenbeck."

"I promise I'll try very hard," Christine was quick to answer. She hugged Harald warmly. She knew there would be no problem with Mother's approval. Mother trusted Harald.

A few days later, Christine stood by the open train window to exchange a few last words with Harald before the train would carry her back to Wiedenbeck. She had rarely left home during her six days Christmas vacation. There was nothing in Bahrenberg that interested her, and being with her family as much as she could eased her conscience about leaving them behind. The air was moist and heavy and smelled of more snow, as Grandfather would say.

"Don't do anything foolish!" Harald brought his face close to the window, straining his neck. The train started to move. Christine could see Harald waving until the train reached the bend. She was relieved. Harald understood her. Tears clouded her eyes as she settled down, and, wrapped in her heavy blanket coat, snuggled into her corner seat. Lulled to sleep by the monotonous chugging of the train she rode into another chapter of her uncertain future.

Chapter 20

The severe winter weather had provided Rita Hartmann with a business opportunity she had been looking for. It was obvious that her husband would not find work. City dwellers were trading their fine china, silver and jewelry for sheep wool and rabbit hair, and Rita Hartmann was the first to open a spinning shop. She had brought her mother's spinning wheel from the attic and acquired three more from farm women. Two refugee women worked several hours daily, depending on the workload. They were paid by receiving a substantial meal per day.

"I can spin," Christine said, looking at the packages of raw wool lined up on the shelf that formerly held Aunt Rita's sewing materials.

"Maybe some time you can help out," Aunt Rita said, but quickly added, "no, it won't work, with school and homework and all your other activities, you won't have time."

Christine's hope for a job were born and crushed at the same moment. She knew there was no way of persuading Aunt Rita who tried to run every minute of her life.

School resumed in the third week of January. Ten days of "coal vacation" had been added because of the cold temperatures and the lack of fuel. Only half of Christine's classmates attended the first day. Wrapped in coats, made from blankets, wearing fur-lined or felt boots, the students huddled in the auditorium listening to Dr. Steiner stressing the need for excellence in studies and devotion to the new tasks ahead in spite of the discouraging winter weather.

"The war to end all wars is behind us, and together we can shape a glorious future," Dr. Steiner declared. He emphasized again the importance of student involvement in eliminating all Nazi and imperialist elements still trying to poison the new society. Some former teachers were gone, new ones had come. No mention was made whether the old ones had left for the west or been fired because of Nazi affiliation. A new wave of refugees had arrived from Russia, expelled ethnic Germans whose families had lived in the Volga region since the 18th century. They spoke little German.

"Our brothers and sisters from Russia have come home and we must help them in their effort to adapt to their new surroundings," Dr. Steiner pointed out.

Christine learned that Sonia Hazek, her "mathematical brain," had been reunited with her family in Cologne on the Rhine. She had left for West Germany just before Christmas. Rosemarie von Hartenstein was not at school the first day, but when she did not appear on the third day, Christine set out to inquire into her whereabouts. Neither teachers nor students had had any recent contact with her. At the school office Christine found out that Rosemarie was still registered.

Under a snow-leaden sky, along the windy and snow-swept Stalin Allee, Christine struggled in her heavy boots toward the suburb where Rosemarie had lived since she and her family had arrived after they were bombed out in Berlin two years earlier.

The entrance was covered with snow, and the absence of footprints told Christine that there had been no visitors for days. Christine knocked on the weather-beaten door. No one answered. She knocked again and listened for even a faint sound. She walked through the white fence gate to the back of the house and called Rosemarie's name, as her eyes traveled along the upper windows for a sign of life. There was none, but she had come so far and she was not about to leave until her purpose was fulfilled.

"There's no one living there anymore," a voice shouted out of an upstairs window of the neighboring house. "They're all gone."

The window slammed closed, and within minutes the front door opened. A woman in her fifties approached Christine. Her eyes were lifeless; her skin sallow, and her thin gray hair was tied in a disorderly bun at the back of her head. A flat, self-rolled cigarette, hung loosely from the corner of her mouth. She threw the cigarette to the ground, spit twice and said in a hoarse voice:

"They're gone. The girl died on Christmas day . . . diphtheria, you know, no medicine, you know, she died horribly, he throat just closed."

Christine felt faint.

"Rosemarie," she whispered. "Rosemarie is dead."

"She isn't dead," the woman said without emotion, just gone. She's probably better off than we are. Who knows what awaits us? Look around you, there is no hope."

She continued to chatter as Christine turned to leave, unwilling to believe what she had just heard.

"If she had been in the west, she would have lived. Here only the big shots get the medicine. And this is supposed to be a socialist country!" the woman shouted. She turned around and waddled back into her house.

Christine, oblivious to the large snowflakes rapidly covering the streets, tumbled along the uneven road surface with burning eyes. "I'll get her, yes, I'll get her, even if it's the last thing I'll ever do." Those words that had cost Miss Olsheimer her teaching position had now become a premonition.

The whirring of the spinning wheels in the workshop welcomed Christine when she returned. Through the open library she could see Uncle Hans, bent over an atlas with a magnifying glass. He looked up, nodded briefly and turned back to the map. Old Senta waddled toward Christine, quickly licked her hand and turned back to her place on the rug by the piano.

A memorial service was scheduled at the school for January 21, eulogizing the "great revolutionary Lenin" on the 22nd anniversary of his death. The stage was draped in black and red, with the red flag, carrying the hammer and sickle emblem, stretched across the wall above the center of the stage. The students filed into the auditorium in a respectful manner, boys to the left side, girls to the right. The sounds of somber music and the Communist anthem filled the large hall. Men in dark suits guided the students to their seats.

Dr. Steiner and several Party officials read prepared speeches. Then followed a film, in German, prepared in Moscow years before, entitled: The Life and Death of a Great Communist.

The narrator told the story of Vladimir Ihlyich Ulyanov, better known as Lenin, born on April 22, 1870, in the town of Simbirsk on the Volga into a middle-class intellectual family of German and Russian background. He told of Lenin's happy childhood in that remote town, and his student years, as rapidly moving pictures depicting the great Volga river delta reeled by.

"He was a bright and rebellious youth," the narrator said. "In his early years he wasn't at all interested in politics, but rather in literature and languages. It was his four year older brother, Alexander, a rather quiet boy, who, as a student, began having political ideas. He was hanged at the age of twenty, together with five of his comrades, for conspiring to assassinate Tsar Alexander III. It was the death of this beloved brother that rushed young Ilhyich into reactionary politics as he vowed to change the social conditions of the people by law rather than through terrorism."

The students watched, seemingly with interest, the account of Lenin's tumultuous political career and its effect on modern Russian history. Lenin was just past fifty when he suffered the first of a series of strokes. The film showed the smiling Lenin, hopeful of recovery, on the eve of January 21, 1924, in the town of Gorki. The next picture showed his physician, Dr. Foerster, bending over the ailing Lenin whose condition had suddenly worsened. Lenin began to breathe in heavy labored gasps. Quickly he went into convulsions.

It was at that moment that a small group of students jumped up and strode defiantly toward the exit.

"We don't have to watch this!" Eberhard Geller, the only surviving son of a local attorney, who had lost three sons in Hitler's war, shouted. "This is a free country now."

A man in a dark suit shot forward.

"No one will leave!" he shouted, blocking the door.

Eberhard pushed him aside, grabbed the door handle but found the door locked.

"You see?" the official hissed. "It's locked."

Eberhard looked around for support from the large audience, but most of the students attempting to leave their seats were restrained by other men. Eberhard and his friends banged against the door, shouting:

"We want out, we want out!"

The film was stopped. The lights went on. The students watched in horror as Russian soldiers with readied guns grabbed the students and led them out of the door that had swiftly been opened from the outside. The heavy door slammed shut. The film resumed as Lenin slipped into eternity.

The students, still numb from shock, watched as the train, bearing Lenin's body in a red coffin, moved slowly from Gorki to Moscow station, where it was picked up by pall bearers and carried for nearly five miles through the streets of Moscow. More than several hundreds of thousand people crowded the sidewalks to pay their last respects to the great man.

Led by the officials, all present in the auditorium rose as an enlargement of Lenin's thin, lifeless face, emphasizing the high cheekbones of his Tartar ancestry, appeared on the screen. The funeral procession on 27 January took Lenin to his final resting place on the Red Square near the

Kremlin, as thousands of sirens, steam whistles, foghorns and bells combined with the roar of guns from ships and cannons in an explosion of sound in a last tribute to the great Communist.

There was a long and heavy silence in the auditorium. When the lights came on, Dr. Steiner rushed onto the stage and said:

"The incident will not be discussed any further!"

All the students, except Eberhard, returned to school the next day. When someone asked them a question, they just shook their heads. Eberhard showed up a week later, ashen-faced, hollow-eyed—silent.

The events of the past days had shocked Christine deeply. The more she turned them over in her mind, the clearer it became to her how helpless she was. Reach high, the whole world is open to you! She shook her head. Phrases! All phrases! How can one live in this atmosphere where the spirit is crushed every day until it fits into a mold? She had to speak to Grandfather. He had to help her to get across the border to the west.

On the first weekend in February, the snow had turned to sleet and rain, Christine set out to visit her grandparents for the first time in the New Year. On Saturday, after school, she ate lunch with the Hartmanns. She cleaned her room in the way it was expected by Aunt Rita, not forgetting that the books had to be arranged in the shelf according to size. She decided to wear her lighter wooden shoes rather than the heavy boots for the long walk to Rebenau. The empty rucksack, ready to supplement the Hartmann's food supply, hung limply on her narrow frame. The rain had stopped, and an occasional patch of blue sky peeked through the high clouds.

She walked to the northern suburb and soon found a ride with a farm woman returning home from her weekly shopping trip to Wiedenbeck. The woman stopped the wagon and nodded. Christine jumped up next to her. No word was spoken. After about half an hour the woman stopped the cart and said:

"I turn in here." She did not look at Christine.

Christine jumped down, a quick thank you. The traffic had subsided since Rebenau was the only remaining town on this side of the border.

Christine looked up at the familiar tall pines on both sides of the road, inhaling their scent in the fresh, moist air that smelled faintly of spring.

The clatter of a horse-drawn wagon made her turn around, the next moment a carriage, drawn by a shiny, well-kept black horse, pulled up to her.

"Please get in!" A Russian officer in is twenties leaned down, smiling.

Christine shook her head.

"No, thanks," she mumbled.

"It's all right," he tried again.

Christine, casting a distrustful glance at the officer, shook her head. He shrugged his shoulders and sped away.

The table was set for dinner when Christine stepped into the Lahrssen kitchen. She quickly washed her hands in the sink and sat down next to Oma Anna, who was cutting slices from a fragrant crusty loaf of bread.

Her satisfaction turned to shock when the door from the hallway opened and a *Vopo*, a member of the dreaded border police, and the new tenant of the Lahrssens, entered and sat down next to Grandfather.

Chapter 21

Lothar Banse was one of the twenty newly trained border guards detailed to Rebenau at the beginning of the year to support the small force of Russian military guards. The recent arrivals were housed with the farmers since no other facilities were available. Neither troops nor farmers liked the arrangement. The soldiers preferred to be with their own kind. The farmers felt spied upon and tried to voice their complaint about the restrictions of their personal freedom, but to no avail.

Grandfather Lahrssen resented the intruder and Lothar Banse, sensing the hostilities, ate silently, hardly lifting his eyes, as he shared the evening meal with the Lahrssens. Oma Anna tried to ease the atmosphere by urging Lothar to eat, to which he responded with a drawn smile. Oma Anna had always taken on the mother role for the young men away from home, as with Jean-Pierre from Marseilles, Jaques from Brussels, Nikolai from Odessa and now Lothar from somewhere in Germany. There was less communication with Lothar, even though they spoke the same language, because he was looked upon as an active enemy. Had the Lahrssens asked him, they might have learned that Lothar had spent five years in the war on various fronts, and when he finally returned, he had found that his family, consisting of his handicapped father, due to a railroad accident, his mother and three younger brothers, had been killed by an air raid on Leipzig. The only skills he ever learned were those of a soldier, since he had rejected becoming a railroad worker like his father. And now he was serving his country again in the way he knew best.

Christine knew the moment she saw Lothar that her chances of crossing the border with Grandfather's help had greatly diminished, but when, after supper, Lothar excused himself and left the house, Christine said:

"Grandfather!"

"Let's go outside and check the horses," Grandfather interrupted. Once outside, he said:

"It's not safe to talk in the house. Who knows if they haven't installed some device to find out what we are talking about and with whom."

They walked past the stables, out of the back gate, into the woods.

"I don't want to be locked up in this big jail, Grandfather, and I need your advice on how to get out."

They walked deeper into the woods. The stillness of the night was interrupted only by the occasional falling of tree branches.

"I suggest you wait until spring," Grandfather finally said. "People are more supportive at that time, they feel more hope. Right now everybody is struggling to get through the winter, with less and less food since the new harvest is so far away. Few people, even in the west, would take on another mouth to feed at this time. Finish up the school year and then we'll plan. By that time we can judge our situation here better. Lothar Banse is not a bad man, but he can't be trusted, at least not yet."

"I heard that the border regulations in the west are easing up, maybe we'll have that here soon, too." Christine suggested.

Grandfather shook his head. "Not here. The Russians hold on to what they have. For them it's a large piece of land towards the west that they can fully control. The Americans were foolish to let the Russians get in that far, but then, they are Allies." He took a deep breath. "The Americans will eventually go home, they wouldn't want to stay on this continent, why should they? They have everything they need in America and much more. Why should they spend all that money to have their troops here?" He paused, stroking his beard. "No, I really don't want to sound pessimistic, but you are right. Soon this will all be one big jail. It seems that the Russian Zone is the only part of Germany that has to pay for Hitler's war." They walked in silence for a long time.

Breakfast on Sundays was at 9:00 o' clock at the Lahrssen's home, and it was an unwritten law that everyone sat down, dressed in their Sunday's bests, on time. Lothar Banse wore his green uniform. The white china with the pink and red rosebuds looked festive on the white linen tablecloth. The freshly sliced gray bread lay on an oval pewter platter. There were jars with gooseberry preserves and applesauce, but the regular bowl with fresh butter had been replaced by margarine bought with ration cards since Lothar Banse had arrived in the house. It was forbidden to churn butter, and Lothar would have had to report the Lahrssens to the authorities had they continued their normal ways.

Oma Anna poured the coffee, made from roasted barley, and Christine passed the milk and sugar around, offering the little silver tray to Grandfather first. Grandfather took a slice of the bread. That signaled the start of the breakfast. Only the clatter of the dishes interrupted the silence.

"It's a sunny day," Grandfather said. "We can take you back to Wiedenbeck this afternoon, Christine. I think Oma Anna would enjoy the ride, too."

"Oh, thank you, Grandfather," Christine said, taking another slice of bread. She noticed Lothar looking at her. He quickly turned his eyes away and blushed. He hurried through his breakfast, coughed embarrassed and getting up, placed his napkin in the silver napkin ring and left the table, closing the door from the outside.

Grandfather looked at Oma Anna and at Christine and back at Oma Anna.

"We didn't say anything wrong, did we?" he asked.

"We didn't say much at all," Oma Anna laughed. "You are getting quite paranoid about the situation, Karl. I think he likes Christine."

A few hours later they drove leisurely along the deserted highway.

"The boys from the west, are they still coming to the dances?" Christine asked.

"Haven't heard a thing," Oma Anna answered, adjusting her shawl. "It's probably too difficult right now with all the new troops, scares people off until they know the new position of the border guards.

Back at the Hartmanns, Christine threw herself into her schoolwork, mainly the studies of English and French. She also volunteered to help out with the refugees, hoping to pick up a few Russian phrases that might be helpful if she got caught by Russian border guards. She could help with the refugees learning German. Her piano and poetry recitation sessions had been postponed until spring because of the winter weather and lack of fuel. She did not mind. There were more important things to do.

The new developments in Wiedenbeck and Rebenau had strengthened Christine's determination to leave not later than spring. Maybe she could establish residence in the west and then help her family to get out before it was too late. And Papa could follow when he returned from the war. She could not confide her plans to the Hartmanns or even to her friend Inge. They must be protected. Leaving the Russian Zone had now become a crime of "depriving the new socialist state of one's working power." An "accomplice," a person who knew about the defector's plans and did not report them, would be severely punished if they were found out. During discussions with Uncle Hans, Christine asked him what he thought about the migration to the west.

"There is a lot to be done here, especially by the young people," he said seriously." We are an occupied country, and now and then incidents occur. But in a few years the foreign powers will leave, and we can rebuild the country in the way we want it to be. True, in the west things improve faster, after all, the Americans are throwing a lot of aid into their zone. America is a rich country." He drew on his pipe. "But we here can say later that we did everything with our own hands, and that's something to be proud of. He leaned back in his large brown leather chair.

"No, I see no reason why people should go over there, leaving everything behind and start anew. Things are getting better here, too, and more and more the Russians are leaving us alone."

Chapter 22

hey came during the night.

"Hartmann, get dressed! You are under arrest!"

Four Russian soldiers stood in the foyer. Uncle Hans, still buttoning his robe, stared in disbelief.

"This must be a mistake!" His voice was trembling. "This must be a mistake!"

"Get dressed! You'll find out over there. Hurry up or—we'll dress you!"

Uncle Hans rushed upstairs, Aunt Rita close behind him. Christine sat at the top of the stairs, shaking.

The four soldiers made themselves comfortable on the antique chairs with the needlepoint covers, wiping their muddy boots on the Persian rugs. Two of them had taken small bags of *makhorka* tobacco and pieces of newspaper from their coat pockets and started to roll cigarettes. They lit them with Uncle Hans' silver table lighter, and the younger one slipped the lighter into his pocket. The other two were just looking around.

"You'd better take your warm coat!" Aunt Rita said as they were coming down the stairs. Uncle Hans was carrying a small bag and reached for his coat in the front closet.

"I'll call Peter in the morning," Aunt Rita said as she helped her husband into his coat. "I am sure everything will be alright."

The soldiers pushed Uncle Hans out of the door and followed him, throwing their half-finished cigarettes on the carpet. They drove off in an American army jeep left behind when the area was turned over to the Russians. The white stars had been painted over by olive drab paint, but were still clearly visible.

Aunt Rita locked the door and fell into a chair.

"I just don't know why they came for him," she mused. "He has never done any harm to anyone—never! And yet, I've always had that fear of the knock on the door in the early morning hours. It has become so . . ."

Her voice trailed off into a sigh.

Christine felt sorry for Aunt Rita, but more for Uncle Hans whom she had come to like and respect.

Aunt Rita got up and said:

"Let's go to bed now, there is nothing we can do right now but get some rest. In the morning I'll call Peter Berger at city hall, I am sure we can get Uncle Hans released." She smiled. "It's good to know people in higher places, even if one doesn't agree with their political convictions."

Christine could not sleep. Thoughts were racing through her mind. What if he really did something wrong? What did she really know about the people she had been living with for about three months? They were good foster parents and had shown their kindness in many ways. No, Uncle Hans' arrest had been a mistake, it had to be. Only four days before a group of Russian soldiers had come to the door, demanding to be let in. Laughing and singing, they had been swinging bottles of vodka, shouting:

"Let's celebrate the end of the war, *Tovarich*." *Tovarich* meant comrade. It was the first Russian word Christine had learned after the Russians had "liberated" Germany.

"Women, get glasses, but fast, we are thirsty!" And they had laughed, throwing their arms around each other and Uncle Hans. They had sat down at the table, and as soon as Aunt Rita had placed the water glasses on the table, they were filled with vodka."

"Here, drink!" One of the soldiers had pushed a glass toward Christine. "Drink it, all of it!"

Christine took a sip. She had never had alcohol before, except for a sip of red wine at her confirmation, and the small amount of vodka burned her tongue."

"Come on—drink up!" One of the soldiers urged.

Christine's eyes filled with tears as she looked at the soldiers. They were not much older than she was.

"I can't," she whispered.

She knew they could force her to drink, pour the vodka down her throat. Her head spun. All the stories she had heard from refugees went through her mind. The soldiers looked at her, then burst out laughing, slapping their knees. They turned to Uncle Hans and Aunt Rita. One of them threw his arm around Uncle Hans, and, with his face close to Uncle Hans' cheek, said:

"We are friends now, *druschba*, no more fighting, peace, friendship, Hitler kaput."

They had stayed until the early morning hours, drinking, laughing, singing, and shouting. They had held on to each other when they left, one of them vomiting on the garden path.

And now they had taken him away.

The next morning Aunt Rita and Christine sat at the breakfast table, beautifully prepared the night before, but neither ate nor drank anything. Aunt Rita looked at the cardigan Uncle Hans had left on the armchair, and tears began rolling down her face. She went to pick it up and placed it on the table in the foyer, taking much care folding it the right way. She returned to the dining room and started taking the unused dishes and silver, returning them to the cupboard.

"Please straighten up a little, Christine, and dust the furniture! I'll work a while in the garden," Aunt Rita said. "It will relax me somewhat."

She walked to the phone in the hall, saying:

"But first I want to call Peter." Her hands trembled as she dialed the number.

"Could I please speak to Peter Berger?" She tried to keep her voice steady. She waited.

"Peter," she said after a while, "something terrible has happened. They picked up Hans last night, would you have any idea where he might be?"

She listened intently while Peter talked, which, to Christine, came across only as a constant low noise.

"All right," Aunt Rita said slowly. "Thank you."

She returned to the table.

"He doesn't know. He says he has no record of Uncle Hans' arrest. It could be a matter strictly of the KGB, and of those cases they have no information at city hall. But he'll try to find out and call us back," she added, trying to control herself. She got up and arranged the flowers in the vase and moved the salt and pepper shaker to the center. "Don't use the vacuum cleaner while I'm in the garden," she said. "We don't want to miss the call."

She went downstairs and Christine heard her open the door to the outside. As Christine dusted, she realized more and more that she really did not know these people. They had told her that he had been a major in the *Wehrmacht*, the German army, but what did he do during the war? She shook her head. He was so soft-spoken, with only cultural and intellectual interests, not at all the German soldier type. No, he was not capable of harming anyone. She searched for some sign of ugliness in him but could find none.

Christine!" It was Aunt Rita calling from the basement, but before Christine could answer, Aunt Rita was in the living room. Her hands were dirty from the soil and her wooden clogs left tracks of dirt all over the rug.

"Do you see that man over there?" She pushed Christine to the window.

A deeply bent figure was walking slowly along the fence, stopping every so often as if in great pain and without strength. He did not look left or right, just to the ground in front of him.

"He told me where Uncle Hans is," her voice tumbled with excitement. "He is at the KGB cellar. This man was released from there this morning. He saw Uncle Hans there and offered to bring a message. He will not give his name or show his face. He told me to keep working while I listened to him as he walked on. He gave me the address. He said there is a little window in the back of the building, the second one left from the back entrance, and that we can take food. Let me heat up some soup and we'll get ready to go right away!"

The streets were deserted. The city looked drab under the gray cloudless sky. After a half-hour walk they saw the building through the tall trees. It looked like the home of a well-to-do family and Christine wondered whether the owners had fled to the west or had been thrown out to make room for the occupiers. There were bullet holes in the lower part of the wall. All window shades were drawn. A child's swing dangled on a long chain from the branch of a huge oak tree that stood in the center of the lawn.

They walked to the back of the house, just as the man had told them to do. They tip-toed to the second window, and Aunt Rita removed the newspaper wrappings from the soup pot while Christine held her handbag. She knocked on the window. It was opened immediately. She whispered "Hartmann," and Uncle Hans appeared almost instantly. She tried to press the pot through the small opening and felt the window being opened more from the inside. Uncle Hans grabbed the pot and urged them at the same time not to come again. He stared at them with vacant eyes.

Relieved that things had gone so well, Christine straightened herself up and, at the same time, felt someone tapping on her shoulder. It was a Russian guard who had followed them.

"Come with me!" he ordered, pointing towards the walkway that led to the front of the building.

"You, too!" He grabbed Aunt Rita by the arm since she had not moved to follow them.

"This forbidden, you know?" He shouted as he took them to the front door. "Take food to prisoners forbidden, you understand?" His voice grew louder: "No good, very bad!"

They arrived at the main entrance where the guard chatted briefly with another soldier. The soldier at the door looked even younger than the one who had arrested the two, eighteen at the most. He smiled sheepishly at Christine but quickly regained his serious attitude when they were led past him. They walked through the foyer into a long hallway.

The guard opened a huge oak wood door at the end of the hall. He closed it immediately behind them. They stood in a large room. The parquet floor looked dull and uncared for. There was a head table with four Russian officers and two civilians seated behind it. On each side of the head table were tables with groups of men in military and civilian clothes.

At the center of the table sat an officer in his mid-forties, with a row of medals across his chest and oversized shoulder bars. He motioned to the women to come forward, and the guard helped by pushing with his rifle butt from behind. The guard said something in Russian to the officer and the officer motioned with his hand that the guard should move back to the door.

"Why did you come here?" the officer asked Aunt Rita.

"My husband is being held here. I'm sure it's a mistake. We brought him some food." Aunt Rita spoke with confidence.

"How did you know he is here?" the officer asked.

"Someone told me."

"Who?"

"I don't know his name."

"When?"

"Today."

"What did he look like?"

"I don't know."

"You don't know?"

"I never saw his face."

The officer looked at the papers that were spread out on the table before him. When he looked up, he fixed his eyes on Aunt Rita and said in an angry tone:

"It is not for you to establish whether your husband's imprisonment is a mistake or not, do you understand? We'll release him when we see fit."

He picked up a pencil, shifted it back and forth while looking downward. He turned to Christine.

"How old are you?"

"Seventeen," Christine replied in a low voice.

"Speak up!" he shouted.

"She's seventeen . . . seventeen . . . she is seventeen . . . !" It was Aunt Rita shouting at the top of her voice. All the time she had been standing slightly behind Christine, but now, with an awkward push of both hands, she tried to move her forward to the head table, all the while screaming:"

"She's seventeen . . . seventeen!"

In the large wood-paneled room with the high ceiling her shrill voice sounded like in a horror movie and seemed to shock everyone.

With a quick motion Christine turned around and stared at her. *My God . . . she's gone insane!* Aunt Rita looked at Christine with triumphant eyes and a chilling smile, like a wolf showing his teeth.

Oh, no! Christine felt faint. *She is trying to trade me in for her husband! I'm going to be raped, perhaps killed . . . oh, no!* She was screaming inside. But Aunt Rita kept smiling, sure that she had found the solution to free her husband.

Christine felt drained of all emotions. She stood there, feeling nothing. An empty shell, she jerked back like a machine and faced the table. The men stared, motionless, in silence.

"Can we go now?" she suddenly heard herself say, shocked at her own voice. The men kept staring. The officer looked at her intently. His face grimaced into a sad smile. He nodded.

Turning to Aunt Rita, he said:

"I should keep you here locked up with your husband! You-you-" He placed his pencil into his shirt pocket and, still looking at Aunt Rita, said, in a voice trembling with anger:

"Don't you ever come back here again!"

He jumped up.

"Now . . . get out!" he shouted, and ran his hand across his forehead.

Chapter 23

A week had passed. There was no word from Uncle Hans. The thin rain, augmented by a gusty wind, pounded against Christine's window. She tried to read but could not concentrate. The scene at the KGB building, and Aunt Rita's screams, she had been so scared. And that officer seemed to feel sorry for her. Maybe he had a daughter her age. And then, how had they gotten out into the street? She could not remember. Only the moment when she had felt Aunt Rita's arm around her shoulder, turning her blood to ice. She had shaken the arm off and walked faster. Aunt Rita tried to keep up with her. Christine started to run and, without thinking, ran faster and faster. She could not feel the rest of her body, only the automatic movements of her legs.

"Wait for me, Christine!" Aunt Rita's scream tore through the air. "Wait for me! Let's go home! Let's talk! I didn't mean it that way. You can't leave me now after all we've done for you. Don't leave me, please . . . !"

Exhausted, Christine had sat down on a bench in the city park. The Lion's Tower, built ten centuries ago, rose behind the duck pond, an ancient symbol of strength and endurance. *I don't ever want to go back there, never!* But where could she go? Not to Grandfather's, not now. Or to Inge? She lived with her mother in a very small room.

Christine had sat down on the stone bench for a long time. As the lights went on in the city, she had gotten up and slowly walked back to the Hartmann house. How she wished that she did not have to go back, but she had no choice.

Aunt Rita had waited by the window and came to the door when she saw Christine opening the garden gate.

"I was so worried about you, Christine," she said in a cold tone. "After all, I am responsible for you. What would I have told your parents had you not come back?"

And Christine had walked past her with downcast eyes. She knew she had to get out of there soon, very soon.

The cuckoo clock struck six times. Christine went downstairs to help Aunt Rita with the supper preparations.

"It seems like you won't be able to go to Rebenau this weekend," Aunt Rita said, contentment in her voice. "It looks like the rain won't let up for days." She probably dreaded being alone in the house and having Christine there was better than being alone, even though there was now little communication between the two.

Christine nodded. She could stay away from Aunt Rita by pretending she had a lot of homework. She could also stop by Inge for a while. And, the first thing she would do on Monday after school, make an appointment to get rid of her braids, she was tired of being treated like a little girl.

Uncle Hans returned a few days later, shrunken and emaciated. He did not talk, only mumbled to himself, shaking his head almost constantly. He stayed in his library all the time and even took his meals there. Every morning he spent over an hour in the bathroom, grooming himself, afterwards he returned to his library to sit and stare out of the window. A few days later workmen came to remove the telephone.

The beautician enjoyed wielding her scissors as she cut off Christine's long, heavy braids. She tried to shape the thick hair to get it ready for the permanent wave, then stopped looking closer at the strands.

"I can't give you a permanent," she said, fingering with the hair. "You have lice." She moved her fingers along the sides of Christine's head. "Not only lice, you have a lot of nits, too." She rushed to the sink and washed her hands.

"You'd better go home right away and get rid of that mess," she suggested. She picked up her scissors and walked to the back, returning after a few minutes. Christine sat pale and speechless in her chair. Finally she said, all strength drained out of her:

"What can I do now?"

"Tell your mother to pour kerosene over your head and wrap towels around, that'll kill them. And when you are clean, come back, and I'll give you the permanent."

She took Christine's hand to make her get up from the chair.

"Come on," she said, now smiling. "It's not the end of the world. Now go home and attack those beasts!" She laughed and walked over to the next customer.

Christine pulled her knitted hat deeply over her head. She was sure that everyone in the street was looking at her.

How awful! Only dirty people had lice. How could she tell Aunt Rita?

Arriving home, she tiptoed to the back of the house, climbed the fence and opened the basement door quietly. She tore her hat off and, in passing the faded mirror above the small sink in the narrow hallway, noticed the chopped off hair. Like a porcupine, she thought. She tried to adjust her hair with her hands, but it resisted. She sat down on a little stool in the laundry room.

Suddenly Aunt Rita stood in front of her. Christine had not heard her coming.

"What's the matter? Is this your new hairdo?"

Noticing Christine's tear-filled eyes, she softened her voice:

"What happened?"

"The electricity went off, so they couldn't give me a permanent today."

"So when do they want you to come back, tomorrow?"

Christine shook her head.

" . . . but when?"

"Some other time," they said.

"That's terrible. They always give you another appointment right away. I'll call . . . oh, no, I can't . . . I'll ride over there."

She turned around and Christine could hear her moving her bicycle out of the storage room. She jumped up.

"Wait, Aunt Rita! Don't go! It's—I—they couldn't give me a permanent because I have—I have—lice."

Aunt Rita stopped and stared and started to move the bicycle back.

"Why didn't you tell me right away?" she asked, when she returned. "Am I such a monster that you are afraid of me? That you can't tell me the truth? You are lucky you did not pick them up earlier, with your schools being used as refugee shelters all the time. Don't worry! We'll take care of this right away. She turned around and strode up the stairs with a purposeful gait.

For days the whole house smelled of kerosene. A few days later Christine returned with her first permanent wave. Not even Christine liked it, but she was a woman now and could face the world in her own way.

A letter arrived from home telling Christine to prepare herself for her return to Bahrenberg. There was still no word from Papa, and the family could not afford the sixty marks for the Hartmanns anymore, especially since Christine had been unable to contribute to the expenses. Besides, Harald's income as a beginning teacher was not enough to support the family. Mother was already a month behind with the payments. Aunt Rita had not said anything; money was not discussed between the Hartmanns and Christine.

The starlings had returned from the south. A few sleek swallows, in their elegant black and white attire, sailed through the air, announcing the arrival of spring. The delicate but hardy snowdrops, heralds of an awakening nature, had long disappeared to make room for crocuses and daffodils. The students were seized by a new vitality. Spring songs sounded from the auditorium through the school building, sung in beautiful harmony by the lower grades with a fervor that lifted even the stuffiest teacher out of apathy.

Christine hummed along, swinging her school bag as she strode along the hall to the exit:

Winter ade, scheiden tut weh.
Aber dein Scheiden macht, dass mir das Herze lacht.
Winter ade—scheiden tut weh.

(Winter, goodbye—Farewells make us cry—
But my heart is filled with joy as I'm singing this goodbye.)

Easter was only two weeks away. The end of the school year signaled Christine's return home. A few days before her former classmate Sigrid Winkler, who lived now just across the border, had invited Christine to spend the Easter holiday with her and her family, "if she could make it." Christine switched to a slower pace, her steps echoing in the hallway. Maybe there would be a chance?

There would be no goodbyes, family and friends must not know. When questioned by authorities they should be able to say that they honestly did not know about her plans to flee to the west, thus they would be protected. This would be her and Grandfather's secret.

"Don't let go of your dream!" She heard him say. "Life is too precious to be wasted."

The bang of the office door hitting the wall interrupted Christine's thoughts. Dr. Steiner, the principal, accompanied by two Russians in uniform, and a man in a black suit rushed into the hall. Talking and gesticulating they charged up the stairs. The elderly secretary came out and closed the door. Something must be going on again, Christine thought, but she left the building without looking back.

She walked along the bicycle path that ran parallel to the railroad tracks. Russian soldiers were guarding open box cars, loaded with typewriters and telephones. One of those telephones probably belonged to the Hartmanns,

Christine thought, soon it will be a welcome addition to an upper class Moscow home.

The next morning the students had to assemble in the auditorium for an announcement by Dr. Steiner. The teachers gathered their students with drawn faces. The students whispered, trying to figure out the reason for another formal gathering. Russian officers and civilian men in black suits sat by the wall; Russian soldiers with weapons were everywhere. Dr. Steiner stepped onto the podium, his face serious.

"Some of our senior students have again tried to sabotage the efforts of our liberators and friends to rebuild this country. They have plotted to destroy the Russian headquarters, the *Kommandantura,* by planting explosives underneath the front entrance. We all bow our heads in shame for having elements in our midst that are so deeply indoctrinated with the Fascist and Imperialist ideology. We must do everything in our power to eliminate these elements. Each student must be on guard and report immediately any conversations and comments against our liberators. We were fortunate to apprehend the criminals at the scene of the crime. They have admitted their guilt and know the consequences.

Dr. Steiner went on to praise the new government and recognize the great progress that had been made in such a short time. He praised the leadership of the Soviet Military Administration for establishing order and discipline that enabled all citizens to look forward to a future of peace and prosperity.

"Together we are building a new nation, and together we shall protect and defend this nation!" He concluded.

He quickly stepped down and left through the back door.

The students filed out of the auditorium in silence and returned to their classes. All week an atmosphere of depression lay over the school. The vacant seats told the students who had been involved in the plot. The fate of the students was never known. They were gone.

As the authorities continued to look for students with revolutionary ideas, distrust among the students became stronger and stronger. Everyone was afraid that a casual comment would be interpreted in the wrong way.

Despite the constant rain Christine decided to go to her grandparents' house the following Saturday. The event at the school had impressed on her that she could not waste any more time. She had to speak with Grandfather.

Without any shelter from a farm wagon traveling the road, she arrived at the farm drenched and shivering.

Grandfather was sitting with his back to the warm tiles, smoking his pipe. Oma Anna was darning Grandfather's socks. Lothar Banse, the border guard, and Wolfgang, who had introduced Christine to the border in fall, were sitting at the round table, playing chess, a plate with *apfelkuchen* between them. They looked up just long enough to nod a hello. The *ersatz kaffee,* made from roasted oats, smelled invitingly and added to the peaceful family scene.

Oma Anna jumped up.

"Oh, Christine, let's get rid of those wet clothes, you'll catch a cold!" She took Christine by the arm and led her to the master bedroom. Within minutes Christine emerged, dressed in a sweater and pants, that belonged to her uncle who was missing in Russia. Oma Anna handed her a pair of wooden clogs. Christine sat down next to Grandfather.

"When you are warmed up, I want to show you the colt that was born yesterday. He's a beauty," Grandfather said, smiling.

"He sure is," Oma Anna acknowledged, handing Christine a cup of peppermint tea and a piece of cake.

Lothar Banse seemed relaxed. Only occasionally did he listen to the sounds from outside, ready to become the tough border guard he was expected to be any time he had to. Grandfather poked in his pipe with a hairpin to extinguish the ashes.

"Now, are you ready to see the foal?" he asked, getting up.

"Of course, let's go!"

Grandfather placed his pipe in the ashtray and buttoned his cardigan. He handed Christine a raincoat from the hook by the kitchen door and took one for himself. Together they walked out to the stables.

The mare turned around and relaxed when she saw Grandfather. The brown foal was struggling to get on his feet and then stood on four thin shaky legs, not daring to move. Grandfather patted the mare on the head and placed his head against her nose. When he turned around he had tears in his eyes. Without speaking he shrugged his shoulders and walked over to the tool shed. They sat down on a bench by the wall. Christine showed him the letter from Sigrid.

"Well, if you want to cross over next weekend." he said.

Christine stared at him.

"But what about Lothar?"

"He has mellowed somewhat," Grandfather spoke in a low voice, looking down at his folded hands. "But I don't trust him yet. Lothar and Wolfgang are good friends, and Lothar does not know that Wolfgang tells us things they talk about."

"No, it's not Lothar that is helping us. It's the widow of a school friend of mine. She and her daughter, whose husband is missing in Russia, live on a farm only three kilometers from here, and about half a kilometer from the border. They occasionally take people across, and she has offered to take you over safely."

They did not speak for a long time.

"I'll miss you very much, but I know it is the best for you," Grandfather said, getting up. "Nobody knows what will happen here, but it can't be good. And you have better chances for a good life in the west. But I must warn you, not all is wonderful in the west, you have to be very careful at all times, but at least you'll be free."

He took Christine's arm.

"Let's go back to the house. They might be wondering what we are plotting."

They placed their raincoats over their heads, and before darting out into the rain, Grandfather said:

"I'll pick you up next Saturday at noon, by nightfall you should be in the west."

Chapter 24

Grandfather was waiting in his horse-drawn wagon not far from the main entrance of the school. Christine, hurried towards him, threw her bundle of clothes on the back and climbed up next to him. The inner turmoil and excitement of the past week had now been channeled into energy necessary to take the final step. She was surprised how calm she was. At this time tomorrow she would be with Sigrid and her family in the British Zone. She had not told them about her plans to stay in the west. Mail was constantly opened and checked, especially between the Soviet Zone and the Western zones.

There had been no goodbyes, her family in Bahrenberg did not know anything about her leaving, but Christine knew that Harald always believed that someday the family would get a message from Christine from the west.

"I shall not take you home," Grandfather said as they were traveling along the asphalted road. "Oma Anna sends her love. I'll drop you off at the Bergdorf crossing."

And he told Christine to follow the country road that would lead almost directly to the Schneider home, the place where she was supposed to go.

They continued in silence.

"This is it! I'll let you off here—quickly, so we don't draw any attention."

A swift embrace, a jump from the wagon, dropping of packages, and Christine disappeared among the pine trees.

She walked along the sandy tracks made by farm vehicles. Tall pines and thick underbrush lined the road on both sides. She was alone in the stillness that was interrupted only occasionally by a falling branch. The birds' twitter had died down. The road, frequently traveled by farmers during the week, was deserted on this Saturday afternoon.

After half an hour Christine saw the thatched roofs of Bergdorf through the pines. She turned right into the narrow walkway that would, Grandfather had told her, lead directly to the Schneider's property.

The clatter of a galloping horse from behind startled her and within seconds the horseman passed so closely, she had to jump into the thicket. He quickly turned around, trying to calm his horse, blocking her way.

"*Documyente pashalusta!*" The harsh Russian command made her tremble and fumble for her identification card. Still shaking, she handed her small white card to the Russian on the horse. It's that officer, she thought, the one that offered me a ride a month ago.

"Where are you going?" he asked in an angry voice.

"I'm visiting my aunt in Bergdorf."

"What's her name?"

"Mrs. Schneider."

The officer, still holding her card and looking at it again, said:

"Mrs. Schneider—your aunt? She could be your grandmother!"

"She is the oldest sister of my father," Christine said, blushing.

"D'you speak Russian?"

"Not yet."

"Don't you learn Russian at school? Or don't you go to school?"

"I'm in the eleventh grade, and we don't have Russian in school, the upper grades have to concentrate on the main subjects for graduation." She added quickly: "But I plan to study it soon."

The officer seemed pleased. He nodded. He pushed the card back into Christine's hand and said:

"You shouldn't be out here alone, it's too dangerous. There are criminal elements all over, especially here near the border."

He turned to leave, stopped again, and asked:

"How long are you staying here?"

"Just this weekend," Christine answered.

Without a word he sped away. Within seconds he was back.

"I'll be at the Schneiders tonight," he said. "I don't like the Schneiders, but I want to talk to you. I want to tell you something about Russia and us Russians. You Germans have the wrong idea about us. Your propaganda made us all look like . . . like . . ." He left without finishing the sentence.

Moments later, Mrs. Schneider opened the fence gate. A large black German shepherd tore at a chain tied to an iron pole by the doghouse.

"So you are Christine," she said, shaking Christine's hand, her voice friendly. Quickly turning serious she whispered:

"What did he want?"

"He . . ." Christine began.

"He's been snooping around here lately," Mrs. Schneider interrupted. "It looks like the word has gotten out that we are helping people across."

"He wants to talk to me tonight and teach me something about Russia," Christine said. "Maybe I should go right back to Grandfather's?"

Mrs. Schneider thought for a moment, holding her chin with her bony thumb and index finger.

"No, you can't do that," she said after a moment. "If he catches you going back tonight, he'll get mad, sure that you had planned to cross to the west." She pushed the bolt into the lock of the gate.

"Come in and take your shoes and coat off, it's warm in the kitchen."

Clara Moehring, Mrs. Schneider's daughter, a rotund woman, wearing a large blue apron and wooden clogs, stood by the iron stove, stirring an aromatic stew. She nodded a greeting but quickly turned back to her cooking.

"Sit down on the sofa, Christine," Mrs. Schneider said. "We'll fix him. You don't need any instructions about Russia. We know it all." She listened for outside sounds and whispered: "I'll make a patient out of you."

She started to bandage Christine's leg almost completely and draped a sheet over Christine after making her lie down, all the while instructing her of her new imaginary accident. She had barely finished when a knock at the door announced the Russian's arrival. Mrs. Schneider rushed to the door.

"Oh, good evening, Sir," she said, bowing slightly. "Do come in!"

"I'm Lt. Ivanov." The lieutenant did not conceal his disgust for the old woman. He looked around and added:

"You have a guest, Miss Bachmann. I came to have a few words with her . . . outside."

"Oh, yes, Sir, but I'm very sorry—please step closer!" Mrs. Schneider chirped, closing the door. She led him into the sparsely furnished living room.

"Most unfortunately—" she bowed again, "Miss Bachmann is inconvenienced tonight. Look at the poor girl!" Mrs. Schneider, a simple woman, always used big words with outsiders. Christine, as instructed, moaned, turning her face to the wall.

"What's the matter?" Lt. Ivanov asked in a suspicious tone.

Mrs. Schneider clasped her hands together.

"You know how city people are in the country, they stumble over everything . . . the water trough in the back! The poor girl, she is so in pain."

She watched Lt. Ivanov. She knew he did not believe the story. But when Christine turned around, tears in her eyes and starting to sob, wiping her nose and eyes on the grayish bed sheet, Lt. Ivanov's expression softened.

"She does seem to be in terrible pain," he said gruffly. "Maybe you should call a doctor." He looked around the room in a way that made Mrs. Schneider feel uncomfortable. Without another word, he left.

Mrs. Schneider fell into the old overstuffed chair.

"He'll be back. He and all of them are watching us. Somebody talked. She locked the door and turned the lights off. She went to the window and looked into the dark night.

"Someone is standing across the street watching our house," she said. A neighbor's dog barked but stopped after a while.

Christine could not sleep. All night long she heard the grandfather clock striking every quarter hour and the cock's crowing before four o'clock. She could hear Mrs. Schneider shuffling around most of the night and was glad, when, at 5:30am, Mrs. Schneider knocked on the door to wake her up. She watched from the kitchen window as the women scurried about with buckets, to and from the stables. Only after all the animals were fed, the cows milked and the milk set out on the bench to be picked up by the milk wagon, did they come into the house to sit down to a breakfast of milk, bread and butter.

"You'll go back to your grandparents today," Mrs. Schneider said, without looking at Christine, as she was spreading the butter on the bread. "Clara will take you back as soon as it is light. I'll bandage your leg right after breakfast, just in case he should show up."

Clara, her face expressionless, did not acknowledge the suggestion.

"You can take Rex for protection," Mrs. Schneider turned to her daughter. "But hold him tight when the patrols come, or they'll shoot him."

An hour later they were on their way. Christine lay stretched out on blankets in the back of the coarse wooden farm wagon, drawn by two black and white cows. Rex was tied next to her on the back of Clara's seat.

Arriving at the back gate of the grandparents' farm, Clara jumped off. She waddled to the house and returned with Grandfather and Oma Anna who helped Christine from the wagon as she briefly explained the bandage. Clara climbed on her seat and drove away without a word.

Oma Anna had barely removed the bandage when Lothar arrived from his night shift. He looked at the three, astonished to find Christine there, said good morning and went to the kitchen to wash up. He soon returned with a cup of coffee and a slice of bread with margarine. He sat down at the round table and turned to Grandfather who had his face cupped in his hands, elbows on the table.

"Is anything the matter, Mr. Lahrssen?" he asked.

Grandfather shook his head, now both hands covering his face.

"Mr. Lahrssen, if there is anything I can do," he coughed embarrassed, glancing at Christine and Oma Anna who had joined them.

"Really, I mean it," Lothar spoke again. "You have given me a home I haven't had for many years, you are my family, and if I could thank you in any way, I—"

"No, I don't think you can help here, Grandfather interrupted. "The fact is that my cousin sent a message from Bergen, which you know is just across the border, to Christine that her mother is very ill. And she wants Christine to come, Christine is her favorite niece."

He took a sip of his coffee and continued:

"Christine came here this morning to see if there is a way that she can cross over to Bergen. She is worried that getting permission would probably take too long. It could be too late for her to see her aunt alive." He paused. "She might even have to stay for a while. We don't know what to do."

Without a word, Lothar got up and left the house.

"He is a good man," Grandfather said. "I don't want him to get into any trouble. The border guards are being watched all the time. He has told Wolfgang, that they even have to watch each other."

Lothar returned two hours later.

"I want to help you," he said in a soft voice. "I've talked to Wolfgang." He paused, lighting a cigarette. "I told him what to do and, Miss Bachmann, you must do exactly as he tells you!" His hands trembled as he blew a few smoke rings into the air.

"I'll be on evening duty tomorrow. Wolfgang will pick you up tomorrow at eight o'clock and will bring you to my post. I'll be on daytime duty on Wednesday, Thursday and Friday for two weeks, if you want to come back then. He gave Christine detailed instructions on how to approach the border on her return.

He went to his room to catch up on his sleep.

At the appointed hour, Christine and Wolfgang walked along the edge of the beech tree forest bordering the cow pastures. Soon they entered the large forest, trying to avoid stepping on dry branches to keep down the noise. They held hands, Wolfgang leading the way in complete darkness.

Neither spoke. They stopped often to listen if they were being followed. As they neared the border, Wolfgang stepped out with confidence. He had traveled that route before.

He looked at his watch with the phosphorous numbers:

"We've made good time. It's only a quarter off."

He pointed to the guardhouse, nestled in a small clearing. He took his wind jacket off, spread it on the ground, and they both sat down, listening in all directions. They heard the rumbling of vehicles along the border, men's voices, and, in the distance, they could see the lights of Dannendorf in the British Zone. Wolfgang strained his eyes to see if there were more people in and around the guardhouse, but he could only determine the constant movements of one shadow in the light of the bare bulb.

"It's five off," he said. "I'll give him a short whistle so he knows we are here."

He pulled the round metal whistle from his pocket and produced a short shrill tone.

Instantly the border came alive. Searchlights went on further down by the highway, trucks and jeeps started rolling. Shouts! Men ran back and forth. Lothar raced out of the guardhouse in the direction where the two had jumped to their feet, standing there, scared. Not knowing what to do.

"You idiot!" Lothar hissed. "You alerted everybody down there. Now get into the tree."

He grabbed Christine by the arm and dragged her behind him as he was racing through the woods toward the narrow stream that was the border. Letting go, he pushed her:

"Run, run, you'll make it! They are busy over there—run!"

Christine jumped across the stream and crawled through the thicket towards the pine woods, her heart pounding. The border was calming down again as she stepped onto the country road that led through the Dannendorf forest. Tense with fear of criminal attacks she continued to run until she reached the first houses of Dannendorf. She sat down on the grass in front of a house, only then did she realize that she had lost her shoes. She got up and walked barefoot the half mile to the Winkler's house.

Chapter 25

The Winklers welcomed Christine like family. Over cups of peppermint tea and bread with lard, they listened as she told them how her well-planned crossing had turned into a nightmare. They asked many questions about life "over there" until long after midnight. The girls had not seen each other since the border was established and talked all night about school, friends, classmates, teachers, occupation problems and family matters. Christine mentioned that she would really like to stay in the west.

When Christine and Sigrid climbed the stairs to the bedroom they would share, way after midnight, Christine realized that all evening she had answered questions, but no mention had been made as to her step into a new life. It was a short night for Sigrid who had to get up at dawn to catch the train to Rheinsdorf where she was now attending high school. Christine slept undisturbed into the late morning, then went downstairs to help Mrs. Winkler with preparations for the mid-day meal. At noon Mr. Winkler was due home for his *Mittagessen,* the noon meal. He was working as a clerk at city hall. In his handsome ruggedness he still looked like the forester he had been for over twenty years.

After taking off his *loden* jacket and washing his hands in the kitchen sink, Mr. Winkler sat down.

"Christine," he began during the meal. "I've tried to get you a residence permit, but since you are under age, and your parents are still in the east, we cannot get that, but I can get you ration cards, illegally, of course. There are many people still on our list that have left our town. We use those ration cards for refugees traveling through, as a sort of carry-over. I can get those for you. But you cannot get permission to attend school here because you cannot become a resident for the reasons I mentioned. Now-" he looked down on his folded hands.

"I have contacted a friend of ours, Mrs. Von Dahlen, whose husband was shot down over England. She is willing to employ you as a maid, without papers, indefinitely, or until regulations ease somewhat. After six months of good behavior, you could become a resident and could apply for a temporary permit to stay. Meanwhile, you have a roof over your head and enough to eat."

Christine nodded relieved. As long as she didn't have to go back, she would do anything: work in the fields, clean house all day. She would wash heaps of laundry, do just anything.

She shook Mr. Winkler's hand.

"Thank you, Mr. Winkler. I'll never forget what you are doing for me."

"Mrs. Von Dahlen is expecting you this afternoon." He gave Christine directions to the Von Dahlen house, got up and threw his jacket over his arm.

"I'll stop by in a few days," he said on leaving. "I think you'll like it there."

Without waiting for Sigrid's return from school in the late afternoon, Christine set out for Buckow, about three kilometers away.

The estate, set back from the street, was surrounded by a park that was just beginning to show the first spring green. It was closed in by a high wrought iron fence. Christine opened the unlocked gate and walked along the graveled path to the front entrance. A young girl in sports clothes opened the heavy oak door and led Christine into the parlor.

"Aunt Elizabeth," she called to the back," the girl is here."

Mrs. von Dahlen appeared. She was a tall, slim woman in her forties. Her dark green wool dress with the beige lace collar enhanced her blond hair, tied in a large bun at the nape of her neck. Smiling, she extended her hand to greet Christine.

"I am glad you are here," she said. "Just come with me, I'll show you around and have you meet everyone here."

They climbed the wide spiral staircase.

"This will be your room," Mrs. Von Dahlen said, opening the polished door. "I'll wait for you in the library while you get ready." She pointed to the room across the hall.

Christine hung her jacket in the large closet that was half-way filled with bags of clothes from which a strong smell of mothballs penetrated the whole room. She opened the windows wide and went to join Mrs. Von Dahlen.

"The girl you met at the door is my niece, Erika, from Hamburg," Mrs. Von Dahlen said as they walked down the stairs. "She's been with us for a while since the food situation in the cities is still very bad. She helps in the house, mainly vacuums and dusts the rooms."

Let's go to the kitchen first," she continued, you will spend much time helping Mrs. Keller. She, too, is a refugee and cooks for us. And when you are not busy in the kitchen, I want you to spend time with Otto."

"Yes, ma'm!" Christine heard herself say. She was a maid already and hadn't even started to work. As she followed Mrs. Von Dahlen she wondered who Otto was, and, yes, she would be a good maid. She would be the best maid they ever had.

"Otto is my son," Mrs. von Dahlen said, half-turning back, "our only child."

Christine nodded.

"Here we are. This is the kitchen. Mrs. Keller, I brought you a helper, her name is Christine."

The stocky woman stopped washing the dishes, wiped her hands on her large apron and shook Christine's hand vigorously.

"You can start right now," she said with a smile, showing large teeth in a round face. "We never run out of work here."

The kitchen on the semi-underground floor was the largest room in the house, with tables, stoves, cutting surfaces, shiny copper pots along the wall, and a lift on which the food was sent upstairs.

They left the kitchen and continued their tour through the living room, dining room, drawing room, smoking room, then upstairs again through the various bedrooms and bathrooms. Mrs. von Dahlen stopped and knocked on one of the doors.

"Come in!" The deep voice from the inside made Christine realize that Otto was older than she had imagined. As Mrs.

von Dahlen opened the door. A boy, about Christine's age, came rolling towards them in a wheelchair.

"Otto, this is Christine." Mrs. Von Dahlen smiled as she introduced the two.

Christine looked into sparkling, deep-blue eyes in a pale face. A bunch of thick dark-brown hair fell over Otto's forehead, almost covering his eyebrow on the left side.

"I'm happy to meet you, Christine!" Otto held out his hand with a smile. "What kind of books do you like?"

"I love most books," she said. She liked Otto already.

"Then we are friends," he beamed. He rolled somewhat back so the two could enter.

"Do you like Somerset Maugham?" Otto asked. Without waiting for an answer he continued:

"I just love his stories. They are so real. Did you know that he is still alive? God, I wish I could meet him some day."

Christine had never heard of Somerset Maugham, his works were not taught in literature classes in the Russian Zone.

"Come over here!" Otto motioned for Christine to follow him. Mrs. Von Dahlen had quietly left the room. Gathering several volumes from a shelf, Otto placed them on the low round table and, not noticing the passing of time, they talked about studies, books, life, teachers and far-away places. Otto had never attended public school since he had contracted polio during the first year of his life.

Mrs. Von Dahlen came to get them to dinner. Otto wheeled himself to the elevator that had been installed in the 150-year old mansion because of his handicap.

"Tomorrow I'll show you the grounds, Christine," Otto said. "You'll be the pilot and I'll be the navigator." He pointed to the handlebars on his wheelchair.

Otto insisted that Christine sit next to him during dinner. Mrs. Von Dahlen seemed pleased that Otto had found someone his age with whom he could communicate. This was more important to her than any housework Christine might do. Otto spent less time in his room as he and Christine explored the park surrounding the villa. Christine, too, felt good in the Von Dahlen house. She did not worry about tomorrow, but she knew she would not stay forever.

Two days later, Mr. Winkler brought a letter for Christine. It had been dropped into his mail slit during the night, probably by somebody that had crossed the border. Christine recognized Grandfather's handwriting but stashed the unopened letter into her apron pocket. It was not right to tend to personal matters during working hours. Alone in her room later in the evening, to the tunes of Glen Miller coming from the old radio Mrs. Von Dahlen had placed on her night table, Christine opened the letter. It read:

"Dear Christine. This letter from your mother was brought to us by Mrs. Hartmann. She was very upset since she did not know what had happened to you. She wants to know if you are coming back, otherwise she'll have to get in touch with your parents to settle the account. Hope all is well. Oma Anna sends her love—Grandfather.

Christine smiled. Let her settle the account, I'm not coming back. Most of my stuff is at Grandfather's anyway.

She opened the letter from home. Mother wrote:

"Dear Christine. Please come home immediately. When you receive this letter, Papa will be home. We were notified by the Red Cross that he is on his way. He is very ill, that's all it said. I urge you to leave as soon as you get this message. My

hands are shaking. I'll close for now. Hurry home. I send you my love, Mother."

Christine stared at the page. No, this was not a trap, this was Mother's handwriting. For hours she lay in bed, staring at the ceiling, thinking, wondering what to do. Sleep took finally over. When she awoke in the early morning hours, she turned off the light and lay in the dark, with her clothes still on, waiting for Mrs. Von Dahlen to knock on the door. She picked up the letter and read it one more time. Mother wanted her home, she needed her. Christine knew what she must do.

After breakfast she asked Mrs. Von Dahlen if she could speak to her alone for a moment. In the library she showed her the letters and told her that she had no choice, she must go home to be with her mother.

"You'd better discuss this with Mr. Winkler," Mrs. Von Dahlen suggested. "With all the crime going on at the border, a young girl should not be forced to cross over alone. Besides, if your mother knew you are here, and safe, she might not insist on your coming back. Your father will be all right after a while."

She paused, and continued:

"I wouldn't want the responsibility of sending you back. What if something happens to you? I could never forgive myself."

She clasped her hands nervously.

"Just talk to Mr. Winkler, but I want you to know that, if you ever come back, our house will always be your home."

They walked back into the dining room where Erika was removing the breakfast dishes. Otto, sensing that something had happened, sat in his wheelchair by the window, waiting. Mrs. Von Dahlen explained Christine's situation.

"Read a lot!" Otto said in a low voice. "And when you come back, we'll have a lot to talk about." He smiled with tear-filled eyes as he shook Christine's hand and wheeled himself out of the room.

The Winklers, surprised to see Christine in the middle of the day, listened intently, but, like Mrs. Von Dahlen, were against Christine's crossing the border alone. Christine, remembering that Lothar Banse would be on guard duty today, assured them that she would be all right.

Eager to arrive in the East in daylight, she set out towards the border. She walked along the country road, past the fields where several farmers were preparing the soil for planting.

As arranged with Lothar Banse, Christine sat on a tree stump and looked at the guardhouse. She waited—and waited. Finally, a border guard stepped out and walked toward the barrier. The guard placed one booted leg on the felled tree underneath the barrier and looked in her direction. Christine raised her hand and waved briefly. He did not wave back. Maybe it isn't Lothar Banse, she thought; maybe his schedule was changed? Maybe he was found out? The guard continued to look but gave no sign. Maybe it is Lothar and he is just being careful? Or maybe he is being watched? She waved again. He went back into the house and returned. Now he was looking at her through a pair of binoculars.

Christine decided to walk closer to the border. As long as she was on West German soil there was nothing he could do, she thought. *Besides, I have an ID card from over there. He should be happy that I am coming back. If this is someone else, I'll tell him the story about my sick aunt in the west who got well because I was there! He'll probably check my papers and wave me right through.*

She walked on the bumpy strip that divided the fields, but decided to walk the last third of the stretch in the ditch, it might be safer. The guard watched her approaching. Christine quickened her step, getting more and more nervous.

Afraid of stumbling she kept her eyes on the ground. At a safe distance from the barrier she looked up and into the eyes of a complete stranger.

With shaking hands she held up her ID card. The guard did not move.

"I'm from the Russian Zone," she said in a low voice. "I just visited a sick aunt." She smiled nervously. "I want to go home. Can't you just let me go through?"

The guard looked nervously left and right.

"I can't talk to you," he hissed. "Go away!"

Christine kept staring at him.

"Go away! Go! Or I have to shoot you. I mean it! But don't run, then I must shoot you . . . !"

He turned around, glancing left and right again, and disappeared in the guard house. Christine saw him looking through the window. She jumped into the ditch and started to run, throwing herself on the ground every so often, her heart pounding; her limbs half-paralyzed with fear. When she reached the forest, it had seemed like an eternity, she looked back. The guard stood now by the entrance, again looking at her with his binoculars.

She sat down on the grass, pondering what to do. She had to go back home. Maybe she could try the cow pasture further up where Wolfgang had crossed several times. He had told her that there are fewer guards in that area.

She set out on the narrow path dividing the potato fields. The tall woods were behind her. The pasture was open, with only small groups of trees and bushes that marked the property of the farmers. She walked towards the border, along the hedge of sloe and blackberry bushes with their budding leaves. There was no marker for the border, no barbed wire. It was common knowledge that the narrow stream was the border. Behind the stream, on the "Russian side," were clusters of small beech and willow trees.

Christine was less than a hundred meters from the stream. She stopped and looked around for any sign of life. She was alone. The air was filled with fright and silence. She had still not calmed down. As she walked forward, she noticed, from the corner of her eye, a slight movement by the tree to her left, but when she looked over, nothing. Should she run, or move more cautiously? She could not decide. Her head was spinning. She took a deep breath to calm herself.

Again she looked over to the left at the gray-brown tree trunks. She stopped. There, next to the one tree, very close, stood another, but that one . . . those red marks! And now she could clearly distinguish the hat and red collar of a Russian uniform. She froze. The Russian stood motionless, not sure whether she had seen him. And then, like lightning, a cape fell to the ground, a boot jumped across the stream. Running, he brought the gun from his shoulder and readied it. Christine could not move. She just stared. In a sudden desperate effort she swung around and started to run. He was coming closer, clearly he wanted to catch her alive rather than shoot her dead. She ran and ran, criss-crossing like a rabbit across the hard grassy surface. A shot whizzed past her ear, and another. She ran sideways and back, upright and bent. This is British occupied territory, he has no right to be here, she thought. The steps had stopped. She looked back. He stood there fumbling with his gun. Shouting in anger, he threw it down, shook his arm at her, picked up the gun and walked back. Two more shots were fired from upstream. Christine threw herself on the ground and fixed her eyes on the border.

Two German border guards joined the Russian as he crossed the stream. Judging from their gesticulating, it seemed they were discussing the incident. Exhausted and disappointed, Christine walked back to the Winkler house.

Mr. Winkler had just returned home when she arrived. After listening to Christine, he said:

"This is it! You have tried. I'll take the responsibility for keeping you here. No one can force you to go back. I will write a letter to your parents and in a few days you go back to the Von Dahlens. I'm sure your parents will understand when they know that you are in good hands."

The same evening a policeman appeared at the Winklers house. He introduced himself as Officer Rhode. He said:

"You are housing a minor from the Russian Zone, Christine Bachmann. I have orders here that she must be returned to her parents. We will accompany her to the border where a team from over there will receive her from us on signature."

"A team! What kind of team—Germans?—Russians?—A Team? Mr. Winkler laughed an angry laugh. "A team! You know what's going on over there. She is not being turned over to a team!"

"I know, I know how you feel," Officer Rhode hastened to say, waving his hand. "But I have orders and that's what I go by."

He fingered his mustache.

"All right. I'll give in somewhat, even though I am not supposed to do that. I'll give you 48 hours to get her across on your own if you have a better way than force. But that's it. I'll be back in 48 hours. Just make sure she is at home or here!"

He strode away, proud that he was part of a new order, even though he was reluctant to turn a young girl over to authorities he couldn't trust at all. But orders were orders, and he would be back in 48 hours.

Chapter 26

Christine stayed with the Winklers while Mr. Winkler tried to find a safe way for her to cross the border, since she insisted that she must go home. Over a few glasses of Scotch Whiskey acquired on the Black Market he talked Officer Rhode into arranging Christine's transfer for Easter Sunday morning, around 10:00, instead of during the night. It was also agreed that Mr. Winkler come along and witness the transfer to see that all went well.

After supper on Saturday before Easter the girls were playing checkers in the living room, Mrs. Winkler was hemming a dress for Sigrid and Mr. Winkler was reading the *Neue Zeitung*, still the only available newspaper.

There was a knock at the door. Mr. Winkler looked up, placed his pipe in the ashtray and walked slowly to the front door.

"It can't be Officer Rhode," he said, puzzled. "We agreed that Christine stay until morning."

All eyes were on him as he waited another moment. He opened the door carefully. He stared at the two women wrapped up to their chins in shawls. He strained his eyes in the dark. One woman removed her shawl.

"I'm Christine's . . ."

"Mrs. Bachmann!" Mr. Winkler exclaimed. "Mrs. Bachmann, please come in!"

Christine came running to the front hall, followed by Sigrid and her mother.

"Mother!" her voice choked with emotion. "Mother, how did you . . . I can't . . ." She sobbed as they embraced for a long while.

"Papa, how is he?"

Mother shook her head and gestured with her hand that she did not want to talk about him at the moment. She turned to Mrs. Schneider. Christine took Mrs. Schneider's arm and brought her forward.

"This is the lady I was telling you about, and now she has brought my mother here."

Mr. Winkler grasped both of Mrs. Schneider's hand.

"You are a very courageous woman, Mrs. Schneider," he said, closing the door behind them.

Mrs. Schneider's face was all wrinkles as she smiled timidly. She made a gesture with her bony hand, indicating that what she was doing was nothing special.

Mrs. Winkler urged the women to sit down while she made room on the table for bread, butter, and the Easter cake she had just finished baking.

"No, no, we are not hungry," Mother declared. "We don't have much time. We just came to get Christine." But she accepted the cup of peppermint tea Sigrid was offering and held it with both hands.

"But please," Mrs. Bachmann," Mr. Winkler interjected.

"We are sorry," Mrs. Schneider said, looking at her deceased husband's metal pocket watch brought out from her trouser pocket. "We are in a hurry. We must be across the border before the guards change."

"But, Mama, is Papa really so sick that I have to go home? You see for yourself how my life is good here, and I'll work hard every day to make it better."

After a long pause, Mother said in a serious tone:

"Christine, you must come back with me. I cannot go home without you!"

Turning to the Winklers, Mother thanked them for all they had done for Christine.

"I am sorry if we have caused you any inconvenience," she said. "But I know you understand."

Christine gathered her belongings and, after hand shaking all around, they stepped into the night.

The darkness hid Christine's tears as the three women walked along the deserted main street in Dannendorf towards the border. Soon they entered the forest to the right and walked in single file along the narrow path away from the highway. Mrs. Schneider led the procession, with Christine in the middle and Mother at the end, probably to insure that Christine would not quietly disappear at the last moment. But she had no such plans. She knew she had to go home with Mother.

The woods were silent. The moist earth smelled of spring. Tomorrow the people of Dannenberg would come here for their Easter Sunday walk to get a glimpse of a *"Vopo,"* an East German border guard, or a patrolling Russian soldier, and realize again, how fortunate they had been to escape Russian occupation. People on both sides of the border never tired of trying to figure out why the border had been established at its present location, right through the fields of these farm communities.

Mrs. Schneider looked up where large clouds moved swiftly across a starlit sky, with the bright moon lighting up the night much too often. They kept walking along the edge of the forest. Mrs. Schneider had instructed them that there would be no talking, that they could walk when the clouds covered the moon, but get down on the ground and not move when the clouds moved away from the moon.

They walked towards the cluster of willow trees, and waded through the narrow stream which held little water. A barbed wire fence had been erected a few feet from the embankment to signal the end of the British Zone. Christine lifted the lower part of the fence for Mother and Mrs. Schneider to crawl through, and then slipped through herself.

Now they were in the Russian Zone. The open field lay before them. The pine forest they must reach was less than a quarter mile across. Christine's heart beat rapidly as she watched the clouds and listened for voices or footsteps. Mrs. Schneider looked around nervously and tried to hurry, at the same time urging the women to reduce the crunching sound of their feet on the dry soil. Any sound seemed magnified in the night. Or was it just Christine's imagination?

Mrs. Schneider stopped and listened.

"Down—don't move!" She urged in a whisper.

There were voices coming from the right, men's voices, getting louder. Russian soldiers! And there they were, just appearing from behind a group of tall trees, hurrying along the country road, chatting and laughing, in the direction of the guard house. *Don't breathe!* Christine strained her eyes as she watched the two soldiers passing at a distance of about 300 yards. *Thank God for another cloud. No, they haven't seen us . . . they are passing, almost gone. I can't see them now but can judge their movements by the trail of their voices. Thank God, that was close. Better stay down for a few more minutes, just to be safe.*

She started to shake as her body released the tension.

They got up to proceed, and then it happened: Mrs. Schneider began to cough. She tried to muffle her cough by pressing her shawl into her mouth, but the more she tried, the more violent became her struggle. Christine listened. The voices had stopped, and so had the footsteps. And then they came running, their heavy boots pounding in quickstep.

"*Stoi! Halt!*" They shouted, wielding their guns: "Hands up!" They were now only a few meters away. The women dropped everything and threw their hands up in the air. When the soldiers realized that there were only women, they relaxed somewhat.

"*Documyente!*" One soldier, about twenty-five years old, shouted, holding out his hand. The women scurried to bring out their identification cards. The soldier looked at them for a while and dropped them into his coat pocket.

"You come with us!" he ordered, turning around and starting to walk. He looked back at Mrs. Schneider who was coughing again. He shouted something in Russian to her, to which she lowered her head without speaking.

They followed the leader across the field to the road in the direction from which the soldiers had come.

"Hurry up!" the younger soldier shouted and pushed Mrs. Schneider as she bent over and coughed again.

The lights of Bergdorf appeared through the tall fir trees.

"I live over there and—"

"I know," interrupted the older guard.

Mrs. Schneider nodded and walked slower.

"I feel very sick, I can't go on," she said.

She stopped, holding her chest, her face distorted with real or pretended pain. "Please let us go home. I'm an old sick woman."

The soldiers continued to walk, turning around occasionally to make sure everyone was following.

"I just don't want YOU to get sick," Mrs. Schneider added.

The leader stopped and turned around. He looked at her with contempt. He thought for a moment, then brought out the ID cards, and said:

"All right, old woman, go home!"

He turned to Mother and said:

"You, too, go home with the sick old woman!"

Mother pretended not to understand. She kept her arm linked with Christine's. The young soldier grabbed her arm and tried to pull her away. But Mother held Christine's arm even tighter.

"I go where my daughter goes," she said firmly.

"Daughter go with us—*rabottatj*—work. You understand?"

He readied his gun.

Mother stared at him with angry eyes. The soldier lowered his gun, turned it around and pushed Mother in the back. Mother sank to the ground, and, in falling, grabbed Christine's leg, pulling her down with her. The soldier pulled Christine's arm to get her away from Mother. Mrs. Schneider had quietly slipped away.

"No! No! No!" Mother's desperate screams tore through the night.

The soldier let go instantly, cursing, probably aware of violating occupation regulations and afraid of possible witnesses summoned by the screams.

"Get up!" the older one grabbed Mother by the arm as Christine helped her. She struggled to her feet, brushing the dirt off her clothing with her hands.

""Get moving!" he shouted. "But fast—*dawai—dawai*! Let's go!"

The *Kommandantura* was a two-story red brick house that once belonged to the mayor of the small town of Letten. He had fled with his family only a day before the Russians arrived, taking only what they could carry in suitcases. The whole courtyard was lit by flood lights.

Mother and Christine followed the soldiers through the tall wrought iron gate. The young Russian guards by the entrance gawked at them. Other soldiers were milling around in the cobblestone courtyard, scanning the newcomers. A few small military vehicles stood along the sides, and a large black sedan was parked in front of the closed entrance door. Every window was lit but the curtains drawn.

They followed the leader around the building to the back door where he picked up a carbide lamp. He led them to a stable building, down the stone steps, into a large cellar. The musty smell from the dirt floor, mixed with human body odor, made the large area feel warmer than it was. A single light bulb hung over the path that was lined, on both sides, with wooden shelves. People of all ages, about twenty-five of them, were stretched out on the wooden planks, their faces toward the path. The guard stopped and motioned for Mother and Christine that this was their assigned place. Mother stepped up and lay down, her head to the wall, but the guard shouted at her to turn around. Christine took her place between another young girl and Mother.

"Where can we—" Christine began.

"Quiet!" shouted the guard, turning back. He then marched off with his lamp and slammed the door.

The cold temperatures and constant activities of new people being brought in kept them awake most of the night. They can't kill us all, Christine thought, trying to relax. She was sound asleep when she felt a tight grip on her arm and a blinding light shining into her eyes.

"Get up!" as soldier shouted. "Get up!" He grabbed the girl next to Christine. "You, too, get up! Let's go! Let's go!"

Mother jumped up.

"I'll go, too," she said, getting up.

"You get back!" The soldier pushed her back with his hands and urged the girls to hurry.

Christine scrambled to her feet. Her legs were shaking as she pushed her feet into the shoes Sigrid had given her. The soldier, with five young girls in tow, walked out of the door, leaving behind a roomful of worried adults.

It was still dark outside. The morning air was moist and fresh, a welcome change after the hours in the stuffy crowded cellar. The girls, hardly awake, trotted behind the soldier to the main building. As they were walking down the hall, one soldier grabbed Christine's arm and said:

"You come with me!"

He led her towards another small corridor to a stairway of about six steps down and along another hall. Christine glanced back to make sure she remembered the exit. She was alone with the soldier who paid her no attention other than making sure she was following him. He opened a door to his left, and pushing her in, growled:

"You *rabottatj* with him—here in kitchen!" He pointed to a big soldier with blond hair and freckles, sitting at the table, peeling potatoes. The soldier grinned as Christine approached, showing a mouthful of decaying teeth. Several buckets of water stood to one side of the table. One bucket, half-way filled with potatoes in murky water, stood on the table by the soldier's side. The rest of the table was covered with potatoes yet to be peeled. The soldier pushed a knife toward Christine and pointed at the potatoes, still grinning.

Christine sat opposite the soldier, with her back to the exit. The kitchen was hot. The soldier, clad only in undershirt and pants, was perspiring heavily. He kept looking at Christine, clearly enjoying her fear and apprehension.

"Name?" he asked in a deep voice.

"Christine."

"Me Misha," he said, pointing at his chest.

Christine, nervously peeling the potatoes, searched for all the Russian words she knew to avoid silence. The soldier laughed out loud, enjoying Christine's struggle.

She had peeled less than twenty potatoes, when the door opened and the guard, who had brought her in, motioned for her to come with him. She followed him up to the second floor to a bathroom where a soldier was washing his shirt in a toilet bowl. The guard picked up a bucket and ordered her to fill it with water from the bathroom faucet, then took her to a bedroom where another girl was already scrubbing the badly soiled parquet floor. On their hands and knees the two girls scrubbed and washed as a group of soldiers watched them from a corner of the room. Within minutes the water was a thick murky liquid and Christine turned to the girl to find out where she could pour it out, since the toilet bowl was still occupied.

"No talk! You go back to your corner!" The guard shouted, stepping forward. Christine looked helplessly at her bucket.

The guard understood. He pointed out of the window where a young woman was just emptying her bucket in the courtyard.

She started to lift the bucket, but without a handle she could grip the bucket by its rim only for a moment. Inch by inch she moved towards the stairway, behind her a group of laughing soldiers, imitating her and egging her on. Her eyes filled with tears of anger and frustration. She finally arrived at the stairs. Suddenly, with a quick motion, two small brown hands grabbed the bucket from her and carried it quickly down the stairs, much to the delight of the other soldiers. A tiny Mongolian soldier almost flew down the stairs with the full bucket. Automatically Christine followed, so did the horde of men behind her. In the courtyard the soldier emptied the bucket with a high swing and handed it back to Christine. The soldiers applauded and made fun of the young soldier who, in turn, clowned around for a while as Christine nodded a quick thank you and rushed back upstairs. She had barely filled her bucket again when the guard appeared again, tapped her on the shoulder and motioned for her to follow him. He led her downstairs to the front hall where about thirty people, including Mother, were standing around or sitting on the ground. Moments later Christine's name was called and she entered the makeshift office. She stared in shock at the officer behind the desk, her legs would not move forward. It was Lt. Ivanov.

"Come here!" he ordered, fingering several ID cards.

"What is your name?"

"Bachmann, Christine Bachmann."

"Where do you live?"

"Bahrenberg, near Magdeburg, Russian Zone."

Lt. Ivanov paused, looking at the papers in front of him.

"What were you doing in the West?"

"I was visiting a sick aunt."

He grinned.

"The west must be swamped with sick aunts," he said.

Christine blushed and bit her lower lip. There was a long silence.

"If I release you today, you'll probably go to the west tomorrow or what are your plans? Or do you have to speak with Mrs. Schneider first?"

"My mother and I must go and see Mrs. Schneider today, she is very ill. We plan to take the train to Magdeburg around noon," Christine said in a low voice.

Lt. Ivanov listened, his mouth drawn. Looking straight at her he said in a low voice.

"Did you really think I believed that trick with the bandage even for one moment?" He shook his head. Christine's face turned a deep red.

"War kills emotions, young people are taught to hate one another. War kills the soul," he said in a low voice.

His face had taken on a painful expression as he looked at Christine again. He shook his head. She stood and waited. Lt. Ivanov looked down on his folded hands.

He straightened himself up, signaled with a small hammer that the guard come in. He told him to bring Mother. He pushed both, Mother's and Christine's cards, toward them without a word.

"You can go now!" he said.

Christine and Mother walked into the hall where the other captives were waiting.

An older woman pressed towards them.

"What happens now?"

"We are going home," Mother said.

"You can leave—Just like that?" She turned to the other people and said, pointing at Christine:

"Wonder what she did, she was in there a long time."

People nodded. The two turned around and walked out of the door.

At twelve noon four Russian soldiers appeared at the Schneider's door.

"We have orders to pick up Christine Bachmann and her mother and put them on the train to Magdeburg," their spokesman said.

As several villagers looked on, the two women, flanked by the soldiers, walked along the dusty road to the station, about half a mile away. The soldiers watched as Christine and Mother climbed the steep train steps into the third class compartment. Mother placed the sparse baggage under the seats as Christine stood by the window, watching the excitement as latecomers scrambled onto the train.

As the train started to move, Christine noticed a lone figure standing away from the station by a tall birch tree. It was Lt. Ivanov. He stood there, like a statue, following the train with his eyes until it disappeared among the pine trees.

Chapter 27

Four weeks had passed since Christine had stepped from the train in Bahrenberg. She was an outcast now, because she had "tried to find a more comfortable life in the decadent west instead of being part of the great beginning of the socialist state." She was now becoming an outcast in her own family.

"Until you become normal again, I cannot let you go back to school, not even to Magdeburg," Papa said during the noon meal while the rest of the family ate the thick potato soup in silence. There was no trace of the pale, weak, helpless prisoner-of-war who had welcomed Christine from his sickbed with open arms, wailing:

"Thank God, we are all together. It's the only way to face this uncertain future."

Less than two weeks before, two education officials had come to the house, asking Papa questions about his past. Yes, he had been a member of the Nazi Party, but not really active. He had always thought of himself as a teacher first.

Papa had also mentioned that he had been fighting in the west and hadn't killed any Russians.

A few days later two officials, Colonel Krotkov and Mr. Wengerov, came again, asking Papa more questions. Papa seemed to have answered them to their satisfaction, and they asked him to sign some papers.

"You may teach again," Mr. Wengerov said, but only the lower grades and provided you are willing to learn and teach Russian."

Papa, who had always been fond of learning foreign languages—he spoke some French and English and had even tried to learn Hebrew in his younger years, nodded enthusiastically. Colonel Krotkov handed him a Russian instruction book for beginners and started Papa on his first lesson. He pointed to the window, saying "*okno,*" then "*stol—karrtina—lampa . . .*" pronouncing the last word as if had a lump in his throat. As Colonel Krotkov pointed at objects around the room, Papa repeated the words, trying hard to imitate Colonel Krotkov's pronunciation.

"*Kharasho!*" the men said, nodding, "*outshen charasho . . .* verry goott!"

Christine appeared with a tray holding cups of tea for the guests.

"This is our daughter Christine," Papa introduced her. "She just returned from northern Germany where she attended school." He did not mention that he had just hauled her back from the west. "She plans to be a teacher like my oldest son," Papa continued proudly. "He's already attending the advanced course in Leipzig."

The men nodded and smiled.

She especially likes working with foreign languages," Papa spoke again.

Colonel Krotkov sat up.

"Do you speak Russian?"

Christine shook her head.

"Not yet, but I have studied English and French. I've always wanted to be a translator and interpreter and travel all over the world."

Papa looked irritated. His daughter was already contaminated by the west.

"And you speak German! And if you add Russian to your languages, you can earn a good salary right here," Colonel Krotkov suggested. "There is a great demand for people with those four languages."

"Or teach those languages after you have attended the teachers institute," Papa added.

Christine looked at Papa and felt she had better not say anymore.

The men rose.

"Don't forget to sign the application for the Party!" Mr. Wengerov advised, pointing to the paper next to the copy of the contract. "Read it carefully! We don't want to force anyone to sign it. Joining the Communist Party is a privilege." He spread out the papers and looked at Papa again with an expression that said: sign that thing or you won't have a job!" Papa signed without a word and handed the papers to Mr.Wengerov.

The men left. Christine, gathering the dishes, glanced at Papa who was reading the copies of the teacher contract and the Party application.

We haven't even recovered from the last "Party," she wanted to scream, and here you are already signing up or the next one. Aloud she said:

"At our school in Wiedenbeck, when we had to watch a film depicting the Life and Death of a Great Communist, Lenin's story, I saw how the Communist Party works."

Papa looked startled.

"What do you mean?" His voice was angry.

Christine stepped back, afraid that she had already said too much.

"It's just . . . it's just that I wouldn't want to be part of a Party like that,"- she stuttered.

He glared at her.

"Let me be the judge of my actions," he shouted. He pulled a plaid handkerchief from his pocket and wiped his forehead.

"Pride and principles don't put bread on the table," he said. "I have a family to feed, and if the Party comes with the job, so be it!"

Papa shoved the papers into the desk drawer and fell into his chair. Christine, feeling a mixture of anger and sympathy, walked over to Papa and put her hand on his arm.

"Papa," she said, trying to stay calm, "we can all still leave. They are closing the border in the north, I've seen it. They have already dismantled the railroad tracks to the north and west. And they are putting up barbed wire. Soon no one will be able to get out."

Papa who had been captured by American troops in the west and turned over to the French, who held him and thousands of German prisoners of war in inhuman conditions under an open sky without food and a minimum of water for months, shook his head.

"I have seen what life over there is about. I cannot give up our home and become part of the huge migration in the West. They have already more people than they can handle. It could mean years of living in a refugee camp." He stared into the distance.

"No," he said, "I have a job now. Life will go on. Politics are done in the big cities, not in the little villages like Bahrenberg. To be honest, I have no choice. I have to feed a family."

Christine knew then that Papa would never leave Bahrenberg. His life was here, good or bad.

During sleepless nights she wondered how she could ever get out of Bahrenberg, with Papa watching her every step, and the border was more than 100 kilometers away. Meals were eaten in silence. Nothing could be said that the younger children could not repeat outside the house.

Christine became a silent robot. In the afternoons she took little Manfred for a walk just to get out. How ugly Bahrenberg was in any season, a sea of stone with stone people. Cobblestone streets, concrete walkways, white washed, cold stone houses, few trees to measure the seasons by.

Holding Manfred's hand, they walked to the Ottersberg Estate, the large compound that had been the American military headquarters many months ago. It was now the Russian *Kommandantura*. The main building was dilapidated. The surrounding fields had been divided up among laborers and refugees who were now working their own land.

Christine and Manfred walked on to the pond that was surrounded by knobby willow trees, stretching their still bare branches straight into the air, like thousands of hands in surrender. On they went to the village hill where the remnants of the Easter bonfire, burned branches and wagon wheels, were strewn about. Together they struggled up, with Manfred rolling backwards more than once. Once they reached the top, the gusty wind played with their hair and clothing as they looked down on the village. Christine brushed the hair out of her face. No, she had never liked this place. It would be easy to leave. But why must she leave her family behind? Her heart was heavy. Whichever she chose, leaving or staying, she would never be really happy. She knew, once she left, she could never come back and they would remain here.

"There has been nothing but tension in this house since you returned," Mother said one morning while Papa was in the classroom. "Sometimes I feel I cannot go on. I weep in the night. I have no solution. I only know that I had no choice but to bring you back here. Papa had ordered me to get you, he had said: Don't you dare come back without her. He did not want to send Harald, because he knew, you would only come back with me. He was so sick then, so unhappy. I was sure your return would keep him from dying."

She looked at Christine with tired moist eyes.

"You are wrong, Christine, treating Papa the way you do. He only has your best interest at heart. He loves you very much. He tells me: "There is no life in that girl anymore, her silence drives me insane. I don't know what she thinks. She never smiles, never talks, never cries."

Christine thought and thought. It seemed like she was poisoning the atmosphere just by being at home. She had to get out before she would not have the strength to do it.

Since Papa did not allow Christine to go back to school, she became a field laborer again. Every morning she went to the Kohler's farm to be detailed to wherever they needed her. As she slid on her knees along the vast sugar beet field to thin out the young plants, she thought of Sigrid and her family in Dannendorf, and of Otto, who was happier in his wheel chair, probably reading Somerset Maugham and H.G. Wells right now.

Harold came home for the summer vacation. He told Christine about his teaching job, about the training, the challenges of guiding Germany's youth to a new and bright future. He could now teach in the classrooms part-time.

"After you go through the basic course, you can prepare yourself to teach foreign languages." He sounded so enthusiastic. He emphasized how proud he was to be part of a new order, of raising a responsible generation, free from prejudice and hatred for their fellowmen, in a free society!"

Christine watched Harald. She had heard speeches like that before. Yes, in Wiedenbeck, at school, the day Eberhard and his friends were dragged away by the new leaders.

The sugar beet fields grew into lavish green ground cover as the wheat fields turned from light green to the color of the sun. Soon Christine and her fellow workers followed the grain cutting machine to gather the grain and tie it into bundles to be dried in the sun and taken home to be threshed.

A few days after Harald had gone back to his teacher institute, Christine asked to speak to Papa.

"I am ready now to apply for the teacher institute. Harald has shown me how wonderful the life of a new teacher can be," she said.

Papa looked surprised, but it made sense that Harald had convinced Christine, they had always been close. He agreed to get the application forms and help her with filling them out.

"And if you join the Party, you can advance faster," he said, pointing out where she would sign."

"I'll wait a while," Christine said. "I want to see first. Besides, we young people are always being told, again and again, to be careful before we sign anything."

Papa nodded.

"So you don't make the mistakes your parents made—I know, I know," he said in a jovial tone, glad that Christine even agreed to sign the application without an argument.

A week later a large envelope arrived, containing more forms to fill out and a lot of propaganda. There was also a paper with Christine's appointment date of August 11 for a medical examination in Magdeburg.

"Christine seems to be a happier person since the papers have been processed," Papa said. "She is probably tired of field labor and is finally looking forward to a new beginning.

August 11. That date was on Christine's mind constantly. It would be the first time Christine would be allowed to leave the house alone. The evening before, as Christine was lying on her bed reading passages of Goethe's Faust, there was a soft knock on the door.

"Christine?"

"Come in, Mother!"

"I thought . . ." Mother began, but her eyes turned to the corner of the little suitcase protruding from underneath the bed. And their eyes met in a long and understanding silence.

Chapter 28

August 11, 1948. The dawn of a clear summer day lay over Bahrenberg. Christine closed the apartment door gently and tiptoed down the stairs. The courtyard door screeched in the early morning stillness. Christine hurried along *Breite Strasse*. By the church, where *Breite Strasse* turns into *Bahnhofsstrasse*, she glanced back. She hoped Papa had not gotten up and watched her from the window as she was walking away with a small suitcase and the carton of books. She could only relax once she was on the train.

Almost a year had passed since she had taken the early morning train to go north to Wiedenbeck to continue her education. Now she was setting out again to begin a new life; not the life her father had planned for her, but her own.

Despite the cool morning air, Christine felt hot. She was restless and tense. She had left without saying goodbye to anyone. Not really. Wasn't it saying goodbye when she tucked the younger children in last night? Or when she had been kind and patient with everyone once she knew her plan? And when this morning she had stuck her head into the bedrooms of her parents and siblings and whispered: "Goodbye, I'm leaving?"

As she walked on the cobblestones, Christine listened for footsteps and voices. She walked faster as perspiration formed on her forehead.

A group of workers stood on the platform, watching the other passengers. Christine walked up to the ticket window of the small brick station building. The rotund station master with the big mustache peered through wire-rimmed glasses, first at her, then at the suitcase. He moved the glasses to the front of his nose and fixed his watery blue eyes on her.

"Going to Grandma's again?" he asked.

Christine shook her head.

"No, I am going to Magdeburg for a physical examination. I am going to be a teacher. Here is my travel permit."

The station master nodded as he took the document and studied it carefully. Christine put her money on the counter.

"One round trip ticket to Magdeburg, please," she said.

The station master elaborately stamped the travel permit and handed her the paper and ticket. He threw another suspicious glance at the suitcase. Christine followed his eyes.

"Oh, that?" she laughed. "That's not my stuff. Remember the Meissners who stayed with us for a while during the Magdeburg bombing raids? Well, they never came to get their stuff, and since I am going to Magdeburg anyway, I thought I'll take it to them. They live near the station."

The station master smiled, flipped down the window and got up to meet the incoming train.

The hooting of the steam engine announced the train as it was coming around the bend. Christine looked once more towards *Bahnhofsstrasse*. She stepped onto the train and cast a last glance at the sleepy town of Bahrenberg, as the train, as if at its last breath, puffed out of the station. The train stopped at several small stations to pick up more workers.

The next three stops would be the Magdeburg industrial suburbs. Christine wondered where the workers spilling out into the barren area were headed. Most of the industrial complex not destroyed by bombings during the war had been dismantled and shipped to Russia.

The train slowed down. She got up, took her baggage from under the seat and moved toward the exit. She knew this was the stop to get off to get closer to the border.

The commuter train to the border area stood on the opposite track. People were boarding from other trains, most probably farm laborers who worked in the border area. Christine followed the other passengers onto the train. She took an aisle seat and scanned the travelers. One woman, wearing a wind jacket and heavy black trousers, moved back and forth among a group of people, talking to them in a low voice. There were no Russian guards on the train. This two-car train, the *Kleinbahn*, was used mainly by farmers.

The train started to move. The passengers looked with bored expressions at the passing landscape.

Christine moved close to the woman whom she judged to be a professional guide for people wanting to cross the border.

"I want to cross over," she whispered. "Can you help me?"

The woman studied Christine.

"Are you alone?"

Christine nodded.

"I'll talk to you in a minute," the woman said, motioning for Christine to return to her seat. Moments later she sat down next to Christine.

"How much money do you have?"

"Six marks."

"Six marks?" the woman said in disbelief.

"But I also have some Chesterfield cigarettes," Christine added quickly.

The woman nodded. After a short while she said:

"I tell you what. I'll take you across. But I have to take these people first. They have paid me a lot of money and I am responsible for their safe crossing. I cannot increase the group, it makes it more dangerous. They already have precise instructions on what to do and I don't have the time right now to go over these with you. We have to get off soon."

She looked out of the window.

"We have to get off here," she said, loud enough for anyone to hear, as the train was slowing down. Turning to Christine she said:

"You'll just wait by the station, I'll get you later. The border is not far, just behind the cluster of farm houses. I'll be back soon."

Christine nodded. She did not trust the woman.

The woman led her group of twelve away from the station onto a farm road. Christine was the only other passenger getting off. She waited several minutes. She followed the group, making sure she could not be seen, as she hid behind trees and bushes. The group entered a small forest and soon came to a clearing. A cluster of stables and a barn surrounded a courtyard with a large dilapidated house. The group disappeared in front of the house.

Shots rang out. Russian voices shouting, people screaming, running feet on the cobblestones, again shouting: "No, no, no . . . *Stoi!* Stop!"

Christine ran to the barn in the back of the house. She pushed on the large door. It flung open. In the semi-darkness she looked into converted living quarters where a woman was lying in bed. In an urgent voice the woman ordered Christine to push her belongings under the bed and put on an apron hanging on a nail on the wall.

"They'll be here any moment. You are my daughter! Come here, quick!"

Christine was still tying the apron strings when the door was pushed open and she stared into the barrel of a gun."

"Border crossers . . . where?" the Russian soldier shouted, rushing towards the women.

"Stay away!" the woman shrieked in Russian. "I am sick, I have tuberculosis. There are no border crossers here, just my daughter. She is taking care of me. Olga! Olga!" The woman grabbed Christine's arm and pulled her on the bed, and, in a mixture of German and Russian, cried: "Olga, help me! I am so in pain."

She wailed and screamed, and tried to get out of bed, as Christine bent down and pushed her back, shouting in German: "Mother, no, no, no, you'll get hurt!"

The soldier retreated, probably afraid of getting sick. While moving backwards toward the door, he poked his rifle under the bed and furniture and pushed a door open that, in this makeshift apartment, held a washtub with potatoes and turnips. He scrambled out of the door, shooting several times into the air before slamming the door shut.

"It's the same every time," the woman said, adjusting her pillows.

She told Christine that she had come from East Prussia with her only surviving son, Erich, seventeen years old, less than a year ago. She had lost her husband and two daughters when they fled from the Russians across Poland, and she became too sick to go on. She spoke Russian fluently.

As they listened to voices, Christine peeked through the small window, she saw several Russian soldiers walking by leading a group of people.

"Oh no! They all got caught—the guide, too!" she said, turning to the woman. "They were on the train with me." She stretched her neck to get a better look.

"*Dawai . . . dawai . . .*!! Hurry up!" the soldiers shouted, as they pushed the people to walk faster. Soon the voices and footsteps faded.

"Erich will be here soon," the woman said. "He works in the sugar factory across the border in the west. He has a special workers pass, he knows all the guards. He can probably help you." She paused. "But please don't ask him to take you across. He is the only person I have left in the world. I am not healthy, I need my son."

Erich looked older than his seventeen years, and he talked like a man who had, through life experiences, grown up too fast.

"I am not surprised about the arrests today," he said, when he heard what had happened, as he was hanging his jacket on the hook where Christine had found the apron. "The guards talked about it last night. They are trying to catch the big fish, the people with large groups. So they rearranged the schedules and routes to mislead the established guides." Erich talked with his mother in Russian for a while and then turned to Christine.

"I'll help you," he said. "I know the guards, I speak their language. In the border towns of East Prussia we grew up with Russian and German, which comes in handy now." He laughed. "But I cannot take you across, just try to help you. If it doesn't work out, I'll bring you back here."

"You want to be in the west in daylight," he continued," so we'd better go."

Christine took off the apron, bent down to Erich's mother and said:

"Thank you very much for helping me. I hope you get well soon." She picked up her belongings and followed Erich out of the door.

The two walked in silence along the narrow path through the pine forest. Christine tried hard to keep up with Erich's big steps.

"How much money do you have?" Erich asked, turning around.

"Six marks," Christine replied.

Erich nodded.

"I hope to find work by this time tomorrow, at some farmer's. I also have two packages of Chesterfield cigarettes."

Erich ran his hands through his pockets.

"Here are sixteen marks," he said, pressing the money into Christine's hand. "That's all I have. You'll need it, especially if you don't find work right away. Now, give me the Chesterfields!"

He stashed the cigarettes into his jacket pocket without a word as they continued to walk. He took the carton from Christine and quickly pushed both, the suitcase and the carton, into the underbrush they were passing. They continued on to the guardhouse.

Christine could not conceal her fright when she saw the two Russian soldiers standing outside the small shack.

The big guy is Leo," Erich whispered. "He says I remind him of his little brother Ivan."

"Oh, little Vanya, what are you bringing us here?" Leo beamed, holding his hand out to Christine.

"This is my cousin Christine," Erich said. "She is visiting us for a few days. So I thought we might come by and say hello."

He brought out the cigarettes and said:

"And we brought you a little present." He handed the cigarettes to Leo.

"Oh, *Amerikanski* cigarettes!" Leo smiled broadly. He opened a package and offered a cigarette to Erich and the other soldier. The soldier ran his finger over it, and commented on the smoothness of the tobacco. He brought it up to his nose, inhaled and smiled. Erich lit them all with his pocket lighter.

"We must go back now," Erich said after a while, shaking hands with the soldiers. Leo shook Christine's hand and said:

"Come and visit us again soon!"

Christine waved once more at the soldiers as she and Erich turned and slowly walked away.

"When we get to the place where your stuff is, we must act quickly," Erich said. "The guards are getting ready for their beat. Just grab your things, run down the embankment and through the creek. The British Zone is 200 meters from here."

Moments later, he cocked his ears, listened intently, shook her hand and said:

"Run now, run!" He quickly walked away.

Christine ran and ran towards the setting sun. She did not know where she was. There were no signs. She finally slowed down when she came to an asphalted road. Exhausted she sat down on a rock by the side of the road.

She started to walk and decided she would ask the first farmer for a lift, regardless of the direction in which he was going. She was in the British Zone. She was in the West. She was free.

A farm wagon drawn by two black and white cows came from the left. She got up and, before she could ask, the farmer stopped and motioned for her to get on.

She was going . . . somewhere.

Senta, The St.
Bernard

Christine, Harald
and Manfred

The Hartmann House

The Polish Weddings

The Lahrssen Farm House

"Little Venice"